Climber's Guide to Devil's Lake

Preparation of this guide
was sponsored by the
Chicago Mountaineering Club

Climber's Guide to Devil's Lake

*William Widule &
Sven Olof Swartling*

THE UNIVERSITY OF WISCONSIN PRESS

Published 1979
The University of Wisconsin Press
114 North Murray Street, Madison, Wisconsin 53715

The University of Wisconsin Press, Ltd.
1 Gower Street, London WC1E 6HA, England

First printing

Printed in the United States of America

For LC CIP information see the colophon

ISBN 0-299-07804-3

CONTENTS

LIST OF ILLUSTRATIONS

EDITOR'S PREFACE

The concept of a comprehensive rock climbing guide to the cliffs surrounding Devil's Lake, Wisconsin, was suggested in the early 1950s by members of the Chicago Mountaineering Club. Several people made starts in this direction, and various notes on climbing routes appeared in the Chicago Mountaineering Club's *Newsletter* from time to time. In 1965 the club published a preliminary edition of Bill Primak's *Guide to the Practice Climbing Areas of the Chicago Mountaineering Club, Devil's Lake Section.* In addition to describing the climbs in the area, it summarized the club's activities in the early 1950s. Primak felt that climbing standards at the lake had, by that time, advanced to a considerable extent and that the earlier descriptions were no longer adequate. His guidebook covered the entire climbing area, but the amount of detail included in the various route descriptions was uneven, with considerable attention given to the older and traditional routes. It is, however, a valuable reference book with much historical information. The only other climbing guide to the area is *Climbers and Hikers Guide to Devil's Lake,* compiled by Errol Morris, edited by David Smith and Roger Zimmerman, and published by the Wisconsin Hoofers in 1970. This book exhaustively describes the climbs on the east portion of the bluffs above the Civilian Conservation Corps camp. Only a few other popular East Bluff climbs and areas are described. The Wisconsin Hoofers generously offered the use of any material in their guidebook in exchange for the use of maps and other information prepared by William Widule and Sven Olof Swartling. The authors have used large segments of the East Bluff descriptions without explicit citation. Unfortunately, because of the additional material included in the

9

present book, much of the exquisite prose style of Errol Morris had to be savagely excised.

This book is a definitive guide to most of the climbs at the lake and contains information from both of the books previously described, with additional information from many individuals. Over a period of several years, the authors have climbed a great many of the routes described. Without the help of many individuals who came forth with much incidental information on routes, history, and so on, however, this guide would not have been so complete. A book of this nature has required the help of many individuals over a long period of time. The role of the general editor has been to coordinate this effort and to consolidate and integrate the various bits and pieces of information into a unified whole.

The authors and the editor are grateful for assistance from the following organizations and individuals: the Wisconsin Hoofers (and in particular David Smith and Roger Zimmerman for use of parts of their guidebook), Chuck and Pat Armstrong, Bill Dietrich, Jim Hagan, Bill Primak, Pete Cleveland, and numerous members of the Chicago Mountaineering Club. They are especially grateful for the support provided by Mrs. Art Campbell and the Art Campbell Memorial Fund. Last but not least, we acknowledge the typing assistance provided by Lois Miller, the final proofreading of Jim Peavler, and the draftsmanship and artwork of Woody Hahn and Kathy Sisson.

George Pokorny
General Editor

Glen Ellyn, Illinois
June 1978

INTRODUCTION

The hard quartzite cliffs at Devil's Lake, Wisconsin, are a geologic anomaly in a region that is better known for its unusual sandstone formations. The rock terrain is hard, with sharp fractures, cracks, ledges, slabs, chimneys, and a variety of rock forms which make this the best rock climbing area in the Midwest. Historically, the popularity of Devil's Lake as a vacation retreat dates back to the mid-1800s, when a number of hotels were built on both the north and south shores for visitors to the lake. Trails above and below the East and West Bluffs have provided enjoyment for hikers and walkers since that time, and, doubtless, scrambling over the boulderfields and lower cliffs was also popular. It was not until 1927, however, that true alpine style rock climbing was introduced to Devil's Lake by Joe and Paul Stettner. Using the traditional climbing techniques of their native Bavarian mountains, the brothers introduced countless numbers of midwesterners to the then unique sport of roped rock climbing.

In 1940 the Chicago Mountaineering Club was established, and the lake bluffs became the preeminent training area for the club's members. With scheduled monthly climbing weekends at Devil's Lake, they trained additional midwesterners in the sport and prepared them for climbing in the mountains. The decade of the 1960s was marked by continuous raising of the standards, accomplished mostly by very young college students. John Gill made some exceedingly difficult climbs in 1960-61, and it was three to four years before anyone approaching his skill came along. Between 1960 and 1966 some fine routes were developed by climbers from the University of Chicago, with the best routes put up by Richard Goldstone and Steve Derenzo. In 1965-68 the Wisconsin Hoofers pushed up several difficult routes on the East Ramparts, which had not been previously climbed. Some of the climbers of that period were Dave and Jim Erickson, Sheldon Smith, Pete Cleveland, and Scott Stewart. The popularity of rock climbing in more recent years has brought still more climbers to the lake, from climbers' organizations to unaffiliated individuals. In addition to rock climbers, more hikers are on the Devil's Lake trails, contributing to the general overcrowding of the park. Unfortunately, this overcrowding has created some problems, and it is hoped that this guidebook will not further contribute to the overcrowding of the climbing areas.

Indeed, serious consideration was given to not publishing this guidebook in order to discourage additional climbers from coming to the lake. It is unclear, however, that guidebooks contribute to overcrowding. It is to be hoped that this book will help to redistribute climbers to areas at the lake that have been unknown and underclimbed in the past. Primarily, we hope that the descriptions and grading of the climbs will help climbers to select climbs that match their skill and ability and permit them to climb in a safer manner.

Every effort has been made to include as many climbs as possible in this guide. There are still many routes waiting to be discovered, and the descriptions given here will eventually be out of date. We would, therefore, be grateful if those who make discoveries, or find errors, would either contact us or communicate with the Chicago Mountaineering Club.

S. O. Swartling
W. Widule

Chicago, Illinois
June 1978

A GEOLOGIC AND NATURAL HISTORY OF THE BARABOO HILLS, WISCONSIN

Patricia K. Armstrong

Devil's Lake, Wisconsin, is one of the most beautiful and unusual areas in the Midwest. Precambrian seas formed the rock of the Baraboo Range, while Pleistocene glaciers shaped the topography and created the lake and its botanical environment. Devil's Lake itself (approximately 1 mile long and 0.6 miles wide) lies in a north-south gap cut by the preglacial Wisconsin River through 500-foot-high bluffs. Cliffs and talus border the lake on three sides. The old river valley trends eastward away from the lake at its south end. Terminal moraines from the last glaciation block the valley east and north of the lake.

The Formation of the Baraboo Quartzite

The story of the Baraboo quartzite began 1.5 billion years ago in the Huronian period of the Precambrian era beneath a quiet sea. Incredible amounts of nearly pure quartz sand were deposited and accumulated at the bottom of this sea until the weight of it all began to press the sediments together into sandstone. Iron oxide and silica (quartz, SiO_2) in solution filled in the spaces and cemented the sand grains together. The pink, red, or purple color resulted from the incorporation of small amounts of iron and manganese. The original formation is thought to have been several miles thick, but weathering through the ages has reduced it to its present 4000-5000 feet.

13

Although most quartzite comes from sandstone that has been heated and pressed to fuse the sand grains together, microscopic study of the structure of the Baraboo quartzite reveals that it solidified slowly, without crystal distortion or high-temperature mineral growth. This means that it is essentially sedimentary instead of metamorphic quartzite. Structures such as ripple marks, bedding planes, cross-current stratification, and pebble layers are perfectly preserved. Ripple marks are especially plentiful around Turk's Head on the West Bluff, and pebble layers can be found east of Devil's Doorway on the East Bluff. Areas in the original sea containing silt were lithified into phyllite, which can be seen as thin, slatey rock, sandwiched between quartzite along the CCC Trail to The Guillotine.

Sandstone is dull and porous and breaks around its cemented sand grains, making rounded holds and sandy ledges. Quartzite, although identical to sandstone in chemical composition, is much harder and breaks across its cemented sand grains, producing a smooth, shiny surface and sharp edges. Thus the cliffs at Devil's Lake are much better for climbing than the sandstones just southeast at Gibralter Rock. On the wall north of the Leaning Tower and cliffs to the east, the cement between the sandgrains has weathered away. This leaves the rock more like sandstone than quartzite in this area, with slightly different climbing problems.

The Building of the Baraboo Range

About 1.45 billion years ago tectonic forces bent, cracked, and folded the huge thickness of Baraboo quartzite into a mountain chain which took the shape of an oval celery dish ten miles wide and twenty-five miles long. It trends west-southwest from Interstate

14

90-94 to a few miles west of Rock Springs, with the village of Baraboo approximately in the middle. The north rim is lower in elevation, with nearly vertical bedding planes visible at the Upper and Lower Narrows of the Baraboo River. The south rim, in which Devil's Lake lies, is higher in elevation and slopes north at about 20-25 degrees. This can be seen when looking across the lake at either the East or the West Bluffs.

The quartzite was extremely brittle and fractured as it was bent, causing both horizontal and vertical cracks. Some slippage along these cracks occurred, as evidenced by pearl-like surfaces on the quartzite. Good examples of these polished surfaces are at The Flatiron and a slanted rock in the Balanced Rock Trail (this rock is now almost entirely covered by a flat rock and concrete). Some of the smaller cracks were subsequently filled in by silica solution and show today as white, quartz-filled veins. A few wider ones have angular pieces of quartzite (breccia) mixed in with the quartz. Examples are visible along the Potholes Trail on the East Bluff.

Tropical Islands in the Cambrian Sea

The next geological event is one of the most interesting. About 600 million years ago, the Baraboo Range, having undergone weathering for nearly a billion years, was submerged in a Cambrian sea. At this time, the quartzite mountain roots (called monadnocks) stood 200 to 600 feet above the water as a tropical atoll. A white-to-tan sand mixed with quartzite blocks, boulders, and gravels eroded from the land and was deposited about these islands.

Studies of the orientation of cross stratifications in the sandstone and in boulder-gravel accumulations around the islands, supported by paleo-magnetic evidence, has led some scientists to postulate that the lagoon and atoll were located in a trade wind zone 10 degrees south of the Cambrian equator.

Fine examples of the cross-bedded Cambrian sandstone with quartzite boulders and gravels can be seen up the Koshawago Spring Valley (southwest of the lake) on the old Chicago Mountaineering Club campground and at Parfrey's Glen (five miles east of the lake). Near the north end of the East Bluff, in the vicinity of Elephant Cave, are other samples of the conglomerate and sandstone formations. Elephant Rock itself bears evidence of wave polishing received when it rested on the shores of the Cambrian sea.

The Missing Record and Mysterious Rivers

Other sandstones, limestones, and dolomites were deposited around the quartzite islands until the Ordovician period some 430 million years ago. These can be seen at Gibralter Rock and other places south and west of the Baraboo Range. From then until the advance of the Pleistocene glaciers one million years ago little is known. If other deposits were laid down, they have since been removed and nothing can be learned about them.

Sometime before the first advance of the glaciers, tremendous rivers cut through the quartzite, making the gaps now filled by the Baraboo River (Upper and Lower Narrows) and Devil's Lake itself. Wells in the south shore campground have failed to reach bedrock 383 feet down, making the old river channel where Devil's Lake lies at least 1000 feet below the present bluff tops.

Water-polished gravels called the Windrow Formation, believed to be Cretaceous (150 million years old), have been found above 1460 feet in elevation on the bluffs. These can be seen near the top of the Pot-

16

holes Trail on the East Bluff. The potholes themselves are an enigma. They had to be formed at the base of a waterfall; they now stand near the top of the bluff. There are even huge boulders bearing potholes back in the woods on top of the East Bluff.

The Pleistocene Glaciers

Several times between a million years ago and the present, glaciers advanced and retreated over the face of the Midwest. In a majority of cases the most recent stage, called the Woodfordian or Cary stage (13,000-16,000 years ago), blotted out all indications of preceding glaciation. The large terminal moraine from this glacier averages 20 to 60 feet high and about 300 feet wide. It snakes its way across Wisconsin and covers half of the Baraboo Range. Prominent forest-covered ridges at the north end of Devil's Lake and across the valley east of the south end of the lake are portions of this terminal moraine. Devil's Lake lies between them, just outside the glaciated area.

Scientists long ago recognized a narrow island of topography in northwestern Illinois, southwestern Wisconsin, northeastern Iowa, and southeastern Minnesota as being very different from the rest of the Midwest. It was long thought to be nonglaciated and was called the Driftless Area. Today many scientists think that the Driftless Area was glaciated by earlier, slow-moving glaciers that left little evidence of their passing. Small, round kettle-ponds west of Baraboo, mixed gravel and sand till-like deposits near Leland, and large boulders out of place, like the pothole rocks on top of the East Bluff, all indicate that glaciers were in the Driftless Area before the Woodfordian era.

In any case, from 12,500 to 30,000 years ago the climate around Devil's Lake was like that in the high Arctic today. Temperatures dropped below freezing

17

several times during the day and night. Water trapped in the cracks and joint planes of the quartzite repeatedly froze and thawed. This frost-plucking or ice-wedging caused huge blocks to topple from the cliffs to make the talus below. Cleopatra's Needle, Turk's Head, Tomahawk Rock, Balanced Rock, and the Devil's Doorway were produced in this manner.

The last glacier advanced over the Baraboo Hills about 13,000 years ago and stood stationary around Devil's Lake for 600 years. It filled in the ancient river valley with two billion cubic feet of debris. Some of it slumped down into the preexisting boulderfields to form the cool depressions along the Grottos Trail. Runoff from the melting ice brought the sand for the swimming beaches and filled the gap between the bluffs and moraines with the waters of Devil's Lake.

Finally the glaciers disappeared and the Wisconsin River (which used to run through the Lower Narrows and Devil's Lake Gap) was left to cut a new channel through the Galesville sandstone at the Dells. Devil's Lake today is several hundred feet above the Wisconsin River. It is forty-five feet deep, is fed by springs and two small creeks, and has no surface runoff. The water is clean and cold and lost by seepage and evaporation. Its beautiful setting, surrounded by pink cliffs and boulderfields, makes many habitats for plants and animals and an attractive place for outdoor sports of all kinds.

Plants and Animals

The uniqueness of the Devil's Lake area owes much to its geologic past. Without the quartzite bluffs and boulderfields, glacial lakes, outwash plains, and moraines there would be less varied habitats for plant and animal life. The area not covered by the most recent glaciation acted as a *refugium* where plants and animals could live while the rest of the area was under ice. These relic communities from the past spread out and met other plant communities reinvading the newly bared glacial landscape from the north and south. About 700 species of vascular plants grow in the area, nearly half of all the species of plants in the whole state.

On top of the bluffs are upland forests, composed primarily of oaks with an understory of red maple. There are also a few hickories and basswoods. On dry southern exposures juniper and rare plants from the south (like prickly pear cactus) can be found. Hill or goat prairies have tall prairie grasses, creamy baptisia, lead-plant, bush-clover, shooting star, yellow star grass, bird's-foot violet, and other plants typical of the grasslands to the south and west of Wisconsin.

The cliffs and boulderfields are home to white pine, paper birch, mountain ash, Virginia creeper and poison ivy vines, red elderberry, alum root, pale corydalis, cup plant, many species of ferns, and hundreds of different mosses and lichens. Narrow glens and canyons hold the most exotic plants, such as hemlocks, yellow birch, blue beech, twisted-stalk, Canada May flower, dwarf ginseng, trailing arbutus, and shining club moss. Cold grottos at the base of the boulderfield have rare northern plants like mountain maple, beaked hazel, shin leaf, oak fern, palm tree, and rose moss. Nearby lowlands have kettle ponds, wet meadows, sand prairies, and tamarack-sphagnum bogs.

Because of the rich assortment of habitats and plants, there are a great number of animals too. Eighty to eighty-five species of birds nest here, and more than one hundred additional species can be seen in migration. The rare peregrine falcon used to nest at the lake. Of particular interest are turkey vultures, pileated woodpeckers, whippoorwills, and winter wrens. Occasionally, bald eagles and ospreys fly over the bluffs.

The largest mammal in Devil's Lake State Park is the white-tailed deer. Gray and red foxes also occur, but are rarely seen. Many small mammals, such as raccoons, woodchucks, squirrels, and chipmunks, are common visitors to the campgrounds. There are thirty kinds of mammals altogether.

Ten to fifteen species of snakes occur, including the beautiful yellow phase of the timber rattlesnake. This snake is not common, however, and is very secretive and rarely seen. There are also nine types of frogs, six types of turtles, and three types of salamanders. In the lake itself are northerns, walleyes, rainbow and brown trout, small and large mouth bass, perch, and several types of panfish.

Vulnerable areas where rare and unusual plants or animals live need to be protected from trampling and overuse. Most people do not recognize rare plants, and indiscriminate hiking and snow-mobiling, cutting firewood, and vandalizing rocks have been very harmful. Efforts should be made to restrict human activities in areas of special scientific interest (like Parfrey's Glen, the Grottos, and the South Bluff). Only in this way can their unique flora, fauna, and geologic attractions be saved for future generations to enjoy.

Man and the Baraboo Hills

At the time that the last glacier was melting from the Baraboo Hills, Paleo Indians were using rock shelters west of the lake. Five hundred generations of Native Americans knew Devil's Lake before the coming of European man. The effigy mound builders built their bird, lynx, and bear mounds around the lake about 600 to 1200 years ago. In historic times the

20

Sioux, Winnebago, Chippewa, and Sauk Indians gave their names and interpretations to the lake.

The Winnebago camped at the lake until 1900 and described the forces which shaped it as a battle between thunderbirds and water spirits. Another legend tells of a great meteorite that produced the Devil's Lake Gap and cliffs. The Winnebago name for the lake was "Ta-wa-cun-chuk-dah" or "Da-wa-kah-char-gra" meaning "Sacred Lake," "Holy Lake," or "Spirit Lake." Other Indians called it "Minni-wau-kan," meaning "Bad Spirit Lake" or "Mystery Lake." Mysterious, musical hammering sounds were supposedly the source of the intrigue.

While doing research on the lichens and mosses of Devil's Lake, I noticed that when the early morning sun warmed the boulderfields, or when the evening shadows crept across the rocks, strange melodious "plonks" occurred on the average of one to two per minute in one small area. These heat expansion-cool contraction sounds, when heard across the distance of the lake and supported by echoes and sounds from other areas, could be the reason for the Indian name.

French voyageurs and missionaries came south from the Great Lakes and north from the Fox River Valley in the 1630s. Settlers began to arrive in the 1830s. Because of the sandiness of the glacial outwash in this area and the rockiness of the Baraboo Range, much of the land was unsuited for farming and thus remained somewhat wild through the years.

The popularity of Devil's Lake as a vacation retreat dates to the mid-1800s. From 1866 to the early 1900s the Minniwauken House (later Cliff House) served thousands of tourists at the north end of the lake. After the railroad was completed in 1873, up to eighteen passenger trains a day went by the lake, nine each way. Side-wheel steamers plied the waters. Kirkland, at the south end of the lake, had more rustic cabins and picnic grounds for the public.

Quarrying operations and proliferating resorts for the elite led many local people to seek state park status for Devil's Lake. After a long battle the lake became Wisconsin's third state park in 1911. The original purchase was $128,000 for 1100 acres. In 1919 the quarry operations were finally removed from the park.

During the 1930s a Civilian Conservation Corps camp was built a mile east of the lake at the south end. It consisted of fifteen buildings and had its own water and sewage systems. Two hundred young men (aged 18-25) arrived at the camp in 1935 and did various jobs throughout the area. They built trails, signs, picnic tables, buildings, and roads. They removed dangerous or infectious plants. They learned about the plants and the park and conducted tours on the bluffs. The CCC program ended in 1941, but the camp served to house employees of a nearby ammunition plant from 1942-45. Four of the original buildings still stand and may be used by scout groups, especially for winter camping.

Today Devil's Lake State Park's six thousand acres host 1.5 million visitors a year. An active naturalist program of hikes and slide shows helps them understand the natural history of the park and the necessity to protect it from the pressures of tourism. In 1971 the park became part of the Ice Age National Scientific Reserve. Steps to eliminate power boats and private cottages have already begun. A reorganization of campgrounds, roads, hiking trails, and interpretive devices is going on right now. Future plans include day use only at the south shore, more trails for hiking and skiing, and a re-routing of many roads. Users of the Midwest's most popular park must be willing to sacrifice their own selfish comforts for the preservation of this unique and beautiful area.

HIKING TRAILS AT DEVIL'S LAKE

Patricia K. Armstrong

Hiking trails of dirt, gravel, or asphalt have been developed by the CCC men and Devil's Lake State Park personnel over the years. Since Devil's Lake became part of the Ice Age National Scientific Reserve, federal funds will help to develop more trails. The interpretation program at the lake includes a nature center and museum at the north shore and many trails around the lake and bluffs. Park naturalists give slide programs and lead nature hikes. There are also two self-guided nature trails with booklets that may be picked up at the nature center.

Some of the park trails are access trails to the climbing areas. Most are for hikers looking for good exercise and fine views. Outside of the park the Sierra Club has developed a narrow trail that runs about fifteen miles, from Honey Creek near Leland to the Klondike Campground in Baxter's Hollow (three miles west of Devil's Lake). There is also a trail into Parfrey's Glen (five miles east of the lake). Because of the fragile nature of the rare plant communities, hikers are advised to stay on foot trails or county roads and not walk cross country.

Since most of the climbing is accessible from the south shore of Devil's Lake, the hiking trails will be discussed beginning from that end of the lake; they have been divided into geographical areas for ease in locating them on the map.

The West Bluff

Existing trails on the West Bluff include the following:

West Bluff Trail—This trail starts at the west side of the south end of the lake and ascends through the woods to the top of the bluff. It follows the rim of the West Bluff and then descends to the north end of the lake. It offers spectacular views of the lake, the Baraboo Valley to the north, the preglacial Wisconsin River valley and Pleistocene glacial moraine to the east, and the Wisconsin River to the southeast. Cleopatra's Needle, Turk's Head, and Prospect Point are landmarks along the way.

Tumbled Rocks Trail—This is an asphalt trail that runs along the bottom of the West Bluff between the south and north lake shores. It follows the west side of the lake through large talus boulders and offers views across the lake to the East Bluff and up the boulderfields to the West Bluff.

Access to climbing areas on the West Bluff are via the Tumbled Rocks Trail and old short-cut trails to the West Bluff Trail.

Proposed trails for the West Bluff will be farther west in the wooded hills, following an old stagecoach trail.

The Southwest Corner of the Lake

Existing trails at the southwest corner of the lake include the following:

Burma Road—Burma Road is a gravel road extension southward from the blacktop road that leads into the south shore of the park. It goes through the woods from the top of the West Bluff.

Koshawago Spring Trail—This primitive trail begins from the gravel driveway just west of the inlet at the southwest corner of the lake. It leads up a rocky valley beside an intermittent stream to Koshawago Spring and then peters out in the wilderness southwest of the South Bluff.

There are no climbing areas southwest of the lake.

Proposed trails for this area will connect the stagecoach trail of the West Bluff with the Koshawago Spring Trail and wilderness to the south and west of the South Bluff.

The South Bluff

There are no existing trails in this area.

There is only one small climbing area on this bluff. It is usually used in winter. There are no access trails.

Future plans for the South Bluff include a trail over the bluff to connect with the Moraine Trail on the east and the Koshawago Spring Trail on the west. The Moraine Trail will run more or less north-south across the South and East Bluffs along the terminal moraine.

The East Bluff

This is the largest bluff, having a north-south trending part along the east side of the lake and an east-west trending part along the north side of the old river valley. Existing trails on the East Bluff include the following:

East Bluff Trail—This trail is on top of the East Bluff and leads from the south end (Balanced Rock Trail) to the north end of the lake. It offers many fine views of Baraboo to the north, the lake below, and the West Bluff. Tomahawk Rock, Elephant Cave, and Elephant Rock are landmarks along this trail.

25

East Bluff Woods Trail—This trail follows the top of the East Bluff from the south to the north end of the lake. It begins and ends in the same area as the East Bluff Trail, but is back in the woods away from the edge of the bluff.

Devil's Doorway Trail—This trail follows the rim of the East Bluff from the lake (Balanced Rock Trail) eastward along the valley. It offers views of the lake and South Bluff as well as Devil's Doorway and some potholes. From the eastern part of this trail one can see the moraine below and Lake Wisconsin in the southeast.

Grottos Trail—This trail runs along the bottom of the East Bluff in the valley. It offers a cool walk through the woods where large depressions called "grottos" occur. There are many nice views of the talus and cliffs above on the East Bluff.

Balanced Rock Trail—This trail begins at the south-east end of the lake, near the railroad tracks, and climbs the talus to the blufftop, where the East Bluff Trail, East Bluff Woods Trail, and Devil's Doorway Trail meet. The Balanced Rock is about two-thirds of the way up the talus. On top of the bluff, park personnel have encouraged the growth of prairie plants. This trail offers good views of the lake and the South and West Bluffs.

Potholes Trail—This trail connects the Grottos Trail and the Devil's Doorway Trail about halfway down the East Bluff. It climbs the talus slope, passes through a cleft in the rocks called Red Rocks, and ends up along many fine potholes worn by a prehistoric waterfall.

CCC Trail—This trail climbs the East Bluff above a former Civilian Conservation Corps camp and turns west along the rim to join the Devil's Doorway Trail. It passes near The Flatiron, The Guillotine, and Leaning Tower and offers fine views of the South Bluff, valley, and Wisconsin River (Lake Wisconsin).

Trail to Group Camp—This trail parallels the road and leads eastward from the south shore campground to the group camp located at the base of the CCC Trail. It goes through the woods with some views of the East Bluff above the trees.

Access trails to the best climbing areas on the East Bluff are the Balanced Rock Trail, Grottos Trail, Potholes Trail, and CCC Trail. Some climbs are also reached from the railroad tracks.

Proposed trails for the East Bluff include part of the Ice Age Trail and the Moraine Trail. The Moraine Trail will follow the terminus of the Woodfordian glacier from the South Bluff across the valley to the East Bluff. From there it will go eastward and north of route 113 and around to the north shore. The Ice Age Trail will be a 600-mile trail connecting the nine parts of the Ice Age National Scientific Reserve throughout the state. In Devil's Lake State Park it will enter from the east along the East Bluff where it joins and becomes part of the Moraine Trail. Then it will follow the East Bluff Woods Trail to the north shore and exit to the northwest along route 123.

The South Shore

Existing trails include:

Landmarks Nature Trail—This trail starts at the Ranger Station on the south shore and follows landmarks around the picnic-camp area and the Grottos Trail to show visitors much of the early history of Devil's Lake State Park. A trail booklet to help the hiker find his way and to explain what he is seeing can be picked up at the nature center on the north shore.

Future hiking and ski trails will be added in this flat valley bottom. The Moraine Trail will cross the valley connecting the South and East Bluffs.

27

The North Shore

Existing trails include:

Pine Tree Nature Trail—This trail starts from the nature center and goes through a pine plantation. Booklets corresponding to numbered posts along the trail are available at the nature center.

Future plans for the north shore include the Ice Age Trail and Moraine Trail as already explained in the discussion of the East Bluff. New ski trails have been completed in the Steinke Basin area.

Devil's Lake State Park presently contains about nine miles of hiking trails. When all proposed trails are completed there will be approximately forty-nine miles of trail. Many of these new trails will be used for ski touring as well as hiking.

GUIDEBOOK USER'S INFORMATION

This guidebook locates and describes the rock climbs in the entire Devil's Lake area, excluding private property. The first part, the East Bluff, describes the climbs on the east side of Devil's Lake, beginning with The Guillotine area at the far eastern edge of the cliffs. The descriptions proceed westward along the cliffs to Balanced Rock, then to the north shore. The second part describes the climbs on the west side of the lake, beginning with the Stettner Rocks at the south end of the lake and proceeding northward along the cliff that constitutes the West Bluff. Since the West Bluff is less accessible than the East Bluff, it has not been climbed as extensively, and a somewhat more detailed description of the trail system is outlined.

The cliffs are further subdivided into climbing areas, and each area description is preceded by a single line contour diagram of that section, with numbers denoting the location of described climbs. The numbers are not always consecutive; sometimes a numbered climb will have an alphabetic qualifier. This slight inconsistency in the numbers results from the way this guidebook has evolved. Routes have been researched for it for over ten years, and the numbering reflects this evolution. Several routes that were listed in the earlier notes were deemed inconsequential, and so were deleted. Some new routes were discovered, however, which were considered worthy of mention, and so were added. These are identified by a number qualified by an alphabetic character.

The shaded portion of the contour indicates that that area is above other parts of the drawing. Ad-

ditional information on the diagram is a directional
arrow indicating compass north (magnetic north) and
a distance scale in feet. Access trails are also shown
on the diagrams, and further orientation of the climbing areas may be obtained by referring to the map of
Devil's Lake.

Much of the early historical climbing at Devil's
Lake is unrecorded anywhere. Many first ascents
must have occurred during this period. Therefore,
because of the great uncertainty regarding the real
first ascent (as opposed to the much practiced first
lead), the descriptions omit mention of the first ascent
or first lead of a route.

Classification of Climbs

The National Climbing Classification System
(NCCS), with one slight modification, is used throughout this guidebook. The slight modification is within
the harder climbs (F9-F10), which makes it possible
to distinguish subclasses. This finer distinction is
possible because of the shortness and accessibility of
the climbs, providing virtually unlimited time for
comparison with other climbs. In the decimal system
this subdivision was often indicated by attaching a
"+" or "—" to the rating of the climb. In this guidebook the classes F9 and F10 are subdivided into A, B,
and C classes, with A being the easiest and C being
the hardest. (For example, F9A vs. F9C.) Following is
a comparison between the NCCS and decimal system.

NCCS	Decimal
F1	1st and 2nd class
F2	3rd class
F3	4th class
F4	5.0-5.2

F5	5.3-5.4
F6	5.5-5.6
F7	5.7
F8	5.8
F9A	5.9—
F9B	5.9
F9C	5.9+
F10A	5.10—
F10B	5.10
F10C	5.10+
A1-A5	A1-A5

Examples of Ratings

These climbs are generally taken to be indicative of their class and are frequently used to compare with other climbs for rating purposes.

F1:	The CCC Trail
F2:	East Bluff's talus slope
F3:	Easy Street
F4:	Anemia
F5:	Beginner's Delight
F6:	Brinton's Crack
F7:	Vacillation
F8:	Birch Tree Crack
F9A:	Upper Diagonal
F9B:	Congratulations
F9C:	Gill's Crack
F10A:	The Black Rib
F10B:	The Flatiron
F10C:	Bagatelle

Although we have attempted to be as uniform as possible in our ratings, differences in individual build, technique, and even preference will make some climbs seem harder, some easier, than their ratings.

Climbing Ethics

More than any other sporting activity, rock climbing and mountaineering need an ethical code of climbing behavior or attitude related to care and respect for the environment. Unlike most other forms of recreation, the very essence of rock climbing and moutaineering depends on the natural scene, a non-renewable resource. The popularity of rock climbing is causing a tremendous human impact upon the cliffs and the surrounding land at Devil's Lake.

The future of climbing is dependent upon a minimum-impact approach. The ecological systems have only a brief growing season between the melting of the last snows and the onset of long harsh winters. Furthermore, the rock formations, which may be broken by the deliberate or thoughtless action of unmindful climbers, cannot mend themselves or recover; they are, in fact, a rather fragile, easily marred, and non-healing climbing medium. Federal and state agencies, as well as private owners, are increasingly concerned about the protection of this environment. In some areas limitations on use are being imposed. Our continuous access to the rock walls at Devil's Lake and elsewhere will depend upon the care with which we treat them.

We therefore urge the climber to consider the cumulative effects of his climbing activities and to tailor his own code of ethics in such a way that traditional mountaineering values are preserved for future generations. We believe that self-restraint and discretion must be employed by each individual in order to preserve the dignity of both our climbing areas and our sport. It is difficult to suggest a set of rules or principles to govern the conduct of people who love freedom—and climb because it makes them feel free. Nevertheless, we are all deeply concerned about the impact on the environment at Devil's Lake of the ever-growing numbers of climbers and hikers. Inasmuch as no specific code of rock climbing ethics exists, we wish to recommend the following interim guidelines be followed as a minimum approach to good environmental conduct.

1. *Climb Clean.* Use restraint in the employment of permanent aid or protection devices such as pitons and bolts, which can permanently deface the rock and degrade the route for subsequent climbers. If such devices are necessary, use the following in descending order of preference: natural formations, chockstones, nuts, pitons, bolts. Nuts have almost completely replaced pitons at Devil's Lake, because in addition to affording adequate protection, they leave the rock intact. On certain routes an occasional "fixed" piton may be encountered. These pitons were left in place to protect the rock and should not be removed.

2. *Use Chalk Sparingly if at all.* Like other climbing aids, the use of chalk is controversial. The usual argument is that it leaves the cliffs unsightly, spoiling the beauty and visual impact. Second, it marks out the holds for the next climber, spoiling the climb for others. Finally, heavy use of chalk is a form of pollution which rains may not wash away for some period of time. If chalk must be used, it should be used sparsely on only the most severe pitches.

3. *Protect the Flora.* The area beneath a climbing line, or a belay stance above the climbing line, is frequently off the trail and may be near flowers or a grassy patch. If the climbing party is large, the impact of many climbing boots may be too much for the delicate micro-environment to bear. This situation is difficult to resolve. If at all possible, try to refrain from overuse of such areas, or stay on the rocks near the start of the climb while awaiting your

33

turn to climb. Also, when hiking or approaching a climb, climbers should stay on the trail as much as possible to minimize the abuse of delicate plant life. Another abuse perpetrated by climbers is the "gardening" of ledges or holds, frequently removing entire plant colonies from the cliff face. This is another case that is difficult to defend, and it is hoped that awareness of the problem will lead to a certain amount of restraint.

4. *Protect the Trees.* Continuous use for belay and rappel anchors can damage and even kill trees. Tree climbing should not be a substitute for routes on rock.

5. *Litter.* Climbers who carry food and beverages with them must be prepared to carry all trash and garbage back to suitable trash containers. Additionally, the concerned climber will pack out litter left behind by the sort of thoughtless person who will always be with us, no matter how high the general level of consciousness becomes.

The place for excrement is in the restroom in the campgrounds; the exercise will do you good.

6. *Be Considerate of Fellow Climbers.* Respect for other climbers should be expressed in a sportsmanlike manner. The following points of exemplary behavior will add to everyone's enjoyment:

a) Be tolerant, understanding, and considerate of others.

b) Avoid arguments.

c) Don't hog climbs; it is very inconsiderate to drop several ropes on nearby climbs and then climb only one route at a time. This may "reserve" other climbs for your party, but it prevents others from climbing in the same area. As Devil's Lake becomes more crowded, climbers must learn to share the limited routes with others.

7. *Observe Devil's Lake Regulations.* The climbing areas described in this guidebook are entirely within Devil's Lake State Park. Therefore, climbers should be familiar with park regulations as outlined in the Visitor's Guide available at Park Headquarters. The guide is a condensation of Chapter 45 of the Wisconsin Administrative Code, which sets forth rules and regulations for use of lands managed by the Department of Natural Resources. Park users have a responsibility to become familiar with these regulations, and abide by them.

Safety

Your enjoyment of climbing at Devil's Lake will be greater if a few simple safety rules are followed.

1. Do not climb alone. Novices should climb with experienced leaders or join a club to learn and practice good technique.

2. Climb with proper foot gear, clothing, and a hardhat.

3. Climb with proper equipment. Roped climbing at Devil's Lake requires a 120-to-150-foot, 7/16-inch nylon climbing rope. More difficult routes will require an assortment of slings, nuts, and carabiners.

4. Do not climb routes that are beyond your ability, and always be prepared to turn back if a climb appears too difficult. Always be able to climb down, never jump.

5. When top-roping always put in two or more anchors. Check anchors and slings frequently for dislodgment and wear.

6. Develop a "feel" for the friction on Devil's Lake quartzite. Remember that wet rocks particularly when lichen-covered, are virtually frictionless.

7. Be aware that wasps may be encountered at any time except during the winter months.

8. Do not dislodge rocks, and if rocks accidentally do fall, warn those below with the call "rock." Try to discourage inconsiderate individuals from throwing rocks.

9. Learn to recognize poison ivy since this plant is growing near some trails and climbing areas.

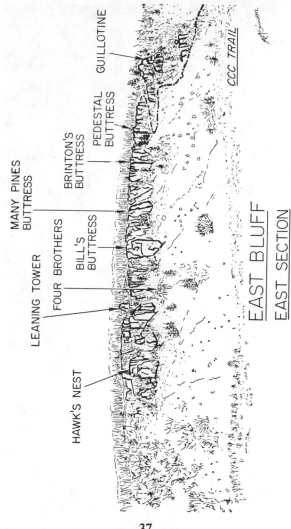

GUILLOTINE

PEDESTAL BUTTRESS

BRINTON'S BUTTRESS

MANY PINES BUTTRESS

FOUR BROTHERS

BILL'S BUTTRESS

LEANING TOWER

HAWK'S NEST

CCC TRAIL

EAST BLUFF
EAST SECTION

37

East Bluff, East Section

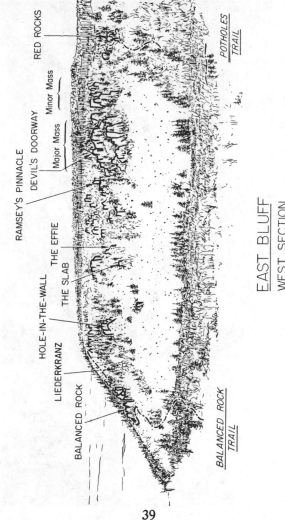

RED ROCKS

POTHOLES
TRAIL

Minor Mass

RAMSEY'S PINNACLE

DEVIL'S DOORWAY

Major Mass

HOLE-IN-THE-WALL

THE EFFIE

THE SLAB

LIEDERKRANZ

BALANCED ROCK

BALANCED ROCK
TRAIL

EAST BLUFF
WEST SECTION

39

East Bluff, West Section

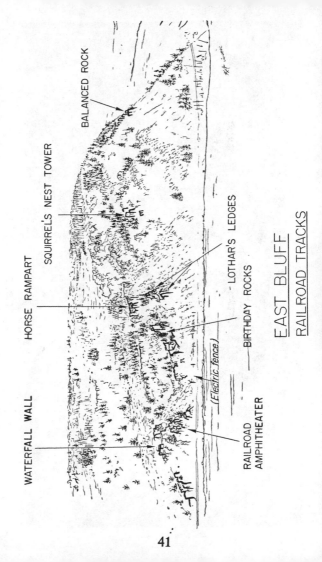

WATERFALL WALL HORSE RAMPART SQUIRREL'S NEST TOWER BALANCED ROCK

EAST BLUFF
RAILROAD TRACKS

LOTHAR'S LEDGES

BIRTHDAY ROCKS

(Electric Fence)

RAILROAD AMPHITHEATER

41

East Bluff, Railroad Tracks

42

THE EAST BLUFF

The climbing areas at Devil's Lake State Park are divided by the lake into the East Bluff and the West Bluff. Both bluffs consist largely of typical alpine talus about 400 feet high, made of rocks ranging in size from small boulders to some as large as a room. Most climbing is done on the broken-up summit cliffs above the talus. In some areas rock outcroppings also appear on the lower slopes, for example along the railroad tracks on the east shore.

Caution should be exercised on unfamiliar routes. Because of the tilt of the rock layers, most ledges on north-facing walls offer poor holds, while walls facing south offer good holds. The Devil's Lake quartzite has poor friction at best and hardly any when wet. This is especially true where the rocks are lichen covered. On sunny days the warm rocks will be covered by swarming wasps. Their nests are usually found in cracks; climbers beware. Another inhabitant of smaller cracks are bats; they and pigeons flushed out of larger cracks and chimneys occasionally give the climber a scare. There is also an abundance of poison ivy in the park.

The East Bluff, by popular convention, is the entire bluff extending south along the east shore of the lake, making a right bend at Balanced Rock and extending eastward to the CCC Trail, near the park boundary. The bluff continues eastward for another mile on private land. Many rock outcroppings east and west of the big quarry, and a sandstone outcropping farther east, can be seen from the road below.

Parking is convenient on the south shore and at the CCC camp one-half mile east of the south shore campground. The campgrounds, as well as the entire park, are very crowded during the summer months.

Three good trails reach up the talus to the top of the bluff: the Balanced Rock Trail, the Potholes Trail, and the CCC Trail. Of course, climbers may reach any part of the bluff by going directly up the boulderfield.

Major Rock Groups of the East Bluff

At the eastern end of the main climbing area, near the CCC Trail, are a group of outcroppings called THE GUILLOTINE. They are the easternmost rocks which are generally climbed. From The Guillotine area, the summit cliff band extends westward almost continuously, with several major buttresses protruding outward and providing extensive climbing routes. This band, the EAST RAMPART, has the highest concentration of climbs of any area at the lake and is surely the most popular climbing area.

Some significant areas along the band include: Brinton's Buttress, Two Pines Buttress, Many Pines Buttress, Bill's Buttress, Leaning Tower, and Hawk's Nest. After a break in the summit band, the cliff resumes west of the Potholes Trail. Here is the largest and most expansive cliff area at Devil's Lake, the DOORWAY ROCKS, which includes the spectacular Devil's Doorway. Continuing westward the outcroppings are discontinuous until the BALANCED ROCK WALL, named after a large boulder perched near the edge. Here the bluff turns abruptly north and follows the shore line.

Viewed from the west side of the lake, the northern leg of the East Bluff has a pronounced diagonal rise to the south in several distinct bands. At the north end of the lake are a few outcroppings in the region of Tomahawk Rock, but they are not extensive or long enough to have excited climbing interest. The lower rock bands are the major structures of climbing inter-

44

est. The lowest northern portion of the band is the RAILROAD AMPHITHEATER and LUMBY RIDGE. Next are the BIRTHDAY ROCKS, HORSE RAMPART, and LOTHAR'S LEDGES.

In general, there is little difference between climbing on either the East Bluff or the West Bluff. The greater concentration of longer, difficult climbs and the well-developed trail system on the East Bluff tend to draw more climbers. The scattering of the rock groups on the West Bluff and the limited trail system make the climbing areas more difficult to locate and therefore less frequented. In the winter the West Bluff may harbor snow for a longer time. It should be recognized that, personal prejudice aside, climbing on either bluff can be equally challenging.

EAST BLUFF ROCK CLIMBS

The Guillotine

The first rock outcroppings along the CCC Trail form a broken ridge on the upper bluff. The climbs are on three main levels: NO SWEAT, GUILLOTINE WALL, and THE GUILLOTINE.

The Guillotine is a cluster of towers standing on the platform above the Guillotine Wall. The name comes from a suggestive wedge-shaped chockstone between two of the towers. A considerable number and variety of short climbs (20-30 feet) are concentrated on the towers and wall below; this is a good area for beginners and larger groups.

Access is by the CCC Trail, which starts ½ mile east of the south shore campground. After ascending the wooded lower bluff in three switchbacks, the CCC Trail passes beneath the first outcrop, No Sweat. The Guillotine is located 100 feet above (north of) No Sweat.

NO SWEAT (Diagram I E)

1 F5. Rib/crack. Ascend easy steps behind tree to west end of No Sweat roof, use crack above to take high step and climb to ledge. A good point to start ascent of the Guillotine ridge.
2 NO SWEAT, F9C. Climb strenuously through notch near center of the roof.
2A NO SWEAT OVERHANG, F10A. Start 5 feet right of No Sweat. Climb past very small 8-inch notch between nose of overhang and No Sweat.
3 F8. East end of No Sweat. Balance from right onto rock projecting from east end, step carefully high left above the roof. Variation, F9B. Start from below and avoid projecting rock.

Diagram I E

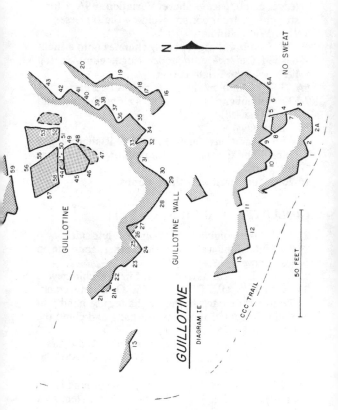

GUILLOTINE

GUILLOTINE

DIAGRAM IE

4 F8. Hand traverse. Start near base of chimney (route 5), traverse 6 feet left with handholds on a ledge, climb to ledge above. Variation, F9A. Climb straight up from bottom avoiding the traverse.

5 F3. Wide chimney.

6 F7. Climb wall right of easy chimney onto a mantelshelf, balance onto upper ledge, climb to top here or around right corner.

6A F9B. Climb cracks 3 feet right of corner.

7-13 A number of 15-foot climbs along the trail and above first ledge.

14 Deleted.

15 F6. Traditional layback, a 15-foot sharp-edged crack along the trail. A faint path branches east at this point.

16-20 Minor wall with short climbs.

GUILLOTINE WALL (Diagram I E)

21 F7. Overhanging nose. Climb on left side.

21A F9B. Climb wall into inside corner, continue on nose above.

22 THE LITTLE THING, F4. Shallow chimney.

23 ANNIE'S OVERHANG, F6. Overhang/crack. Climb a thin crack to the overhang, use hand jam hold in left crack above the overhang and climb the right crack to top.

24 POISON IVY, F5. Corner, small holds at first.

25 RHUS TOXICODENDRON REDICANS, F8. Climb, staying right of corner.

26 LEVITATION, F5. Getting off the ground is the hardest part. Climb onto left side of slab, stem past first overhang, finish on left wall.

27 LEVITATION RIGHT SIDE, F6. Start at right side of slab and continue fairly straight up about 5 feet right of the inside corner. Variation, F10A. Start same as Levitation Right Side. At

8 feet stretch far right and move up, avoiding holds on Labor Pains, finish straight up to top.

28 LABOR PAINS, F9C. Start at left limit of undercut section; the difficulty is concentrated in the first 6 feet.

29 F7. Corner. Use a layback and pinch hold on right side to gain first corner ledge, continue up the corner onto next small ledge, a mantelshelf problem.

30 BROKEN BOULDERS, F4. Crack starting from niche. Variation. Begin farther right on a slanting ledge.

31 THE LAYBACK, F5. Very strenuous when done as a pure layback, jamming left leg in the crack is an easier technique.

32 F6. Corner.

33 BEGINNER'S CHIMNEY, F4.

34 BEGINNER'S NOSE, F4.

35 BEGINNER'S FACE, F5. Climb 4 feet onto first ledge, then up left corner. Variation, F6. Go more directly up middle and right side of the face.

36-43 East end of the Guillotine Wall.

THE GUILLOTINE (Diagram I E)

44 GUILLOTINE WEST, F4. Chimney. Climb by bridging back and feet or by stemming; the latter method is neater. Optional finish: from upper chockstone traverse underneath top overhang on south tower.

45 F5. Low-level traverse 2 feet off ground.

46 F7. Overhanging crack.

47 F4. Ledges, easy except for retable at top.

48 F5. Corner with small balance holds.

49 BAREFOOT CRACK, F4. Face/cracks. Here is a climb to practice placing hardware.

50 GUILLOTINE EAST, F4. Chimney, easy stemming practice.

51 F8. Narrow face with small holds.

52 THE GOPHER, F7. Work up right side of corner onto small face holds, then grab for top.

53 F7. Crack starting behind block.

54 Deleted.

55 F4. Chimney, tapered to provide any width.

56 F5. Corner, climb straight up. Variation, F4. Traverse right-hand crack.

57 ANARCHIST CRACK, F5. Crack leading to upper ledge. Harder if right corner is out of bounds.

58 DECAPITATION, F7. Climb wall just right of corner to upper ledge, then climb on small holds to top.

East Rampart (Diagram II E)

This cliff band extends for ¼ mile along the summit of the East Bluff, averaging about 80 feet in height. It is generally considered to have the finest climbing at Devil's Lake. Access is by the CCC Trail. After climbing past the first rock outcrop (No Sweat), the trail skirts a scenic boulderfield and turns abruptly left at the base of a short wall (The Monster). The wall has two notorious climbs, The Monster and The Thing. The main summit cliff is reached just above; here a climber's path splits off to the left (west) along the base of the rampart, while the regular trail goes up right around the east end.

The description below follows the major buttresses (projecting cliff sections) as you walk west along the rampart. The selected routes have interesting climbing as well as good protection (excepting the most severe climbs).

D'Arcy's Buttress is at the east end of the rampart. Recommended routes: Last Gasp, F8; Easy Overhang, F5; Zig-Zag, F6. *The End,* a huge out-leaning

Diagram II E

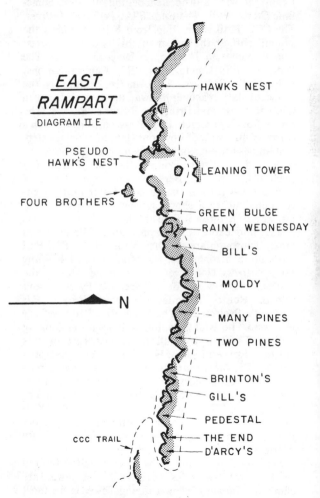

tombstone with a deep cleft behind. Routes: Sometime Crack, F9B; The End, F9A. *Pedestal Buttress.* The CCC Trail, ascending from below, reaches the summit cliff at the corner of this buttress. Routes: The Stretcher, F9A; Upper Diagonal, F9A; The Pedestal, F5; Condolences, F7; Congratulations, F9B. *Gill's Buttress.* A distinctive feature is the Boyscout slab, reaching halfway up the wall between Gill's Buttress and Brinton's Buttress. Routes: The Spine, F5; Gill's Crack, F9C; Boyscout, F4. *Brinton's Buttress.* Just west of Boyscout slab. Some giant stepping stones are encountered when walking around the base of the buttress. Routes: Brinton's Crack, F6; Brinton's Direct, F8; Berkeley, F6.

Two Pines Buttress is the next major buttress encountered (after a short, somewhat broken section just west of Brinton's). The east face of Two Pines has a fairly noticeable rippled appearance. Climbs in this area: Thoroughfare, F10A; Vacillation, F7; Full Stop, F6; Schizophrenia, F6; Moderation, F4. *Many Pines Buttress.* Note several pines on the ledges of the east side. The west side is exceptionally steep and smooth. Routes: Anemia, F4; Peter's Project, F7; Michael's Project, F7; The Black Rib, F10A. *Moldy Buttress.* The west side has a high rotten-looking ceiling. There is a small tower just east of this buttress. Routes: Lichen, F4; Tibia Crack, F8; Horticulture, F5. *Bill's Buttress.* A broad deep-based buttress. There is a decided dip in the trail as it passes below. Routes: The Cheatah, F9B; Push-Mi Pull-Yu, F6; Agnostic, F7; Coatimundi Crack, F6. *Rainy Wednesday Tower.* The top of this buttress is isolated from the bluff top by a gap 20 feet deep. Routes: False Alarm Jam, F6; Double Overhang, F5.

Leaning Tower is along the summit trail at the top of the bluff. All sides of this 30-foot tower are climbed. The gully below Leaning Tower is the most definite break in the length of the East Rampart. Below the gully there is a small outcrop, the *Four Brothers.* It is a good area for beginning leaders, offering a multitude of nut placements. *Pseudo Hawk's Nest* is the section immediately west of Leaning Tower access gully. Routes: The Pretzel, F6; Beginner's Delight, F5; Hero's Fright, F7; Bloody Mary, F8. *Hawk's Nest* is a large impressive wall at the west end of the main climbing area. The wall is steep and smooth, especially near the bottom where there is just one point of weakness (The Funnel) leading to the two recommended F6 variations. Routes: Happy Hunting Grounds, F10A; The Funnel/Bucket Brigade, F6; The Ramp, F6; Vivisection, F10A; Anomie, F8; Charybdis, F7; Coronary, F7.

THE MONSTER to PEDESTAL BUTTRESS (Diagram III E)

1 THE FLATIRON, F10B. This is a ghastly John Gill boulder problem (every area has them). Start where the trail reaches the base of a subsidiary wall just below the main summit cliff, on a smooth slab of rock 15 feet high. Climb up the center of the slab. An easier variation on sides.

1A F9A. Start at top of The Flatiron, and climb the short wall above.

2 THE MONSTER, F9B. A short unfriendly crack. Start in a shallow alcove in the overhanging wall. Climb to top of alcove then up crack above.

3 THE THING, F7. A typical Devil's Lake paradox —how can it be so hard when it looks so easy? Start at base of chimney or groove (an approach from left or right is preferable to direct attack), climb groove to top.

4 F8. Climb left corner of the wall.

4A F8. Climb cracks in the middle of face.

Diagram III E

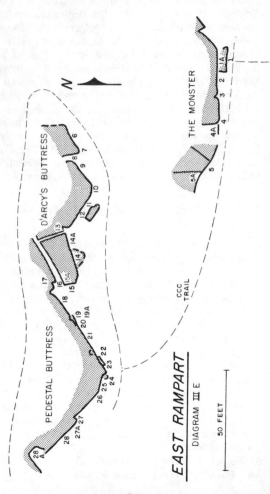

EAST RAMPART
DIAGRAM III E

50 FEET

5 THE BODY SNATCHER, F7. It would be well not to fall traversing out from the chimney. Start below shallow chimney capped by an overhang. Climb crack at left to ledge at base of the chimney, up chimney, step left and up to top.

5A F7. Start on bench just left of The Body Snatcher, climb flake and crack. (There is another crack 5 feet left of the flake.)

6 CEMETERY WALL, F6. Short boulder problem. Start in center of face.

7 SHIP'S PROW, F6. Jutting nose. Likened to keel-hauling.

8 30-SECOND CRACK, F4. For those who are bothered by exposure.

9 D'ARCY'S WALL, F8. Named for Ray D'Arcy, who never was able to make the last crux reach. Start on right side of the wall, near the inside corner. Climb left to approximate center of the wall (A), then up to top. (A) GRAND TRAVERSE, F8. Traverse left around corner to Last Gasp.

10 LAST GASP, F8. Many a climber has grasped the final ledge only to fall off from utter exhaustion. Start in the pit slightly left of corner (starting from adjacent rocks is strictly frowned upon). Struggle up to ledge, continue close to corner to top.

11 EASY OVERHANG, F5. Offers an introductory course in the use of buckets. Climb to ledge behind large block, traverse to right crack, negotiate overhang and on to top.

12 ZIG-ZAG, F6. This line follows left crack behind the block. Climb to ledge as above, zig left and zag right to clear overhang, continue crack to top. Try to be one of Devil's Lake select few who didn't use the Linden tree.

13 DARKNESS AT NOON, F4. Stygian chimney.

14 SOMETIME CRACK, F9B. When queried about whether they lead this cliff, climbers typically give the evasive response "sometime." Start on slab 15 feet high at base of overhanging jam crack. Climb jam to intersection with horizontal crack (A), traverse 5 feet right, then up to top. (NOTE: On top rope, watch for severe pendulum.) (A) BLOW-UP, F9C. Hand traverse left to corner, up crack to top. SOMETIME LEFT, F10B. Start left of crack, climb overhanging wall to Blow-Up, traverse right to Sometime Crack, then straight up.

14A SOMETIME CRACK RIGHT SIDE, F10A. Thin crack on right side of the overhanging wall. Climb crack to alcove then up left to regular route.

15 THE END, F9A. One's last lead at Devil's Lake? Start on block outside the deep cleft, traverse right onto the narrow overhanging wall, climb wall (if lucky) to top. Variation, F9C. Start at bottom, taking care to avoid the block used above.

15A END OF THE END, F9A. Start on same block as The End, climb corner above (i.e., left corner of The End).

16 CHIMNEY'S END, F5. Deep cleft behind The End, can be ascended as a chimney. You can walk up through base of this cleft or through another that meets it at right angles (Darkness at Noon).

17 THE BEGINNING, F7. Groove or V-chimney. There are F4 ledges just left of the groove.

18 THE STRETCHER, F9A. Start on smooth face 10 feet right of Birch Tree Crack. A couple of long reaching moves, then up, up, up to top. Variation, F10B. Same start but climb straight up for 15 feet to join Stretcher route.

19 BIRCH TREE CRACK, F8. This is a one-move climb. Without the proper technique it becomes a no-move retreat. The birch tree that once grew here could not stand the continual abuse of falling climbers. Start on ledge 10 feet up, climb into alcove and up crack to top.

19A THE HOURGLASS, F10B. Start this climb between Upper Diagonal and Birch Tree Crack, then straight up face 5 feet left of Birch Tree Crack. SWEATSHOP, F10A. Climb wall, staying between Upper and Lower Diagonal.

20 UPPER DIAGONAL, F9A. Strenuous but well protected. Start on same ledge as Birch Tree Crack. Climb left into the diagonal crack, follow crack to top.

21 LOWER DIAGONAL, F8. Offers experience in placing protection on the run. Start near base of large pine tree, up to (lower) diagonal crack, climb crack to ledge (A) at left corner, exit left. (A) THE TRICK, F8. Finish by attacking wall directly above the ledge, a bit left of corner.

22 THE PEDESTAL, F5. A traditional two-pitch climb. Start below detached flake, climb right edge to top of the flake (pedestal), traverse left (crux) around corner to hidden triangular belay ledge. Second pitch: traverse farther left to pine tree, climb crack to upper ledge from which several finishes are possible.

23 CONDOLENCES, F7. A straighter version of The Pedestal, a strength climb. Start under left edge of the flake. Climb crack and overhang, then up onto (crux) the flake. Traverse left to corner, climb corner past bulges to ledge (same ledge as on Lower Diagonal). Variation, F10A. Same start as Condolences. At 10 feet climb short face (sharp fingerholds) just left of Pedestal flake.

24 GOLDEN LEDGES, F10A. The gold is fools gold, as well as the ledges. Start just left of corner, climb into open book (groove) on the corner and up to the traverse on The Pedestal.

25 ALL THE WAY, F10C. No easy moves on this climb. Start in groove 5 feet right of Congratulations, then straight up face to Pedestal belay ledge, continue straight up.

26 CONGRATULATIONS, F9B. One of the classic "hard" routes, the scene of many falls. Climb the steep crack leading to pine tree. NOTE: there is an A4 aid route between Congratulations and Ironmongers.

27 IRONMONGERS, F7. Start at base of tree, climb into alcove, step left and up the crack in the face to ledge. PINE BOX, F9B. Climb straight up from the alcove.

27A IRONMONGERS SUPER DIRECT, F10A. Start 5 feet left of Ironmongers. Everything but the corner is legal.

28 LETHE, F7. Climb slabby wall past overhang to ledge. An easy crack leads to top.

28A Easy (F4) climbs in upper recess.

GILL'S BUTTRESS to TWO PINES BUTTRESS (Diagram IV E)

29 FANTASY, F9A. Start at base of smooth wall. Climb up 10 feet, then a little right (8 feet) and back left into notch at top of the wall. Variation, F10B. Climb straight up to top notch.

30 THE SPINE, F5. Deep groove or chimney. Start at crack on left side, climb into the groove and up. Harder (F6) if you eliminate right wall of the groove.

31 ACID ROCK, F10C. Smooth high wall left of The Spine. Start on top of A-Frame block, on right side of the wall. Climb until 10 feet above the good ledge, traverse left and up to fixed pin near

Diagram IV E

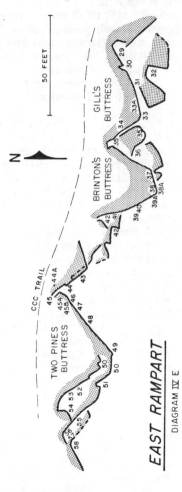

EAST RAMPART

DIAGRAM IV E

left corner, continue near corner then right to finish at center of the wall.

32 THE A-FRAME, F7. A peculiar cave-like chimney beneath the main walls. Climb up high inside then move out horizontally to the south.

33 GILL'S NOSE, F10B. Start at base of corner, climb face just left of the corner. At the top, a harder variation is climbing on the nose.

33A F10A. Climb wall between Gill's Nose and Gill's Crack.

34 GILL'S CRACK, F9C. Start halfway up Boyscout slab, climb crack in right-hand wall.

35 BOYSCOUT, F4. A standard "easy" route often crammed with boy scouts. Climb slab (many variations) to base of large chimney, up chimney to top.

36 CHEAP THRILLS, F10C. Start at left edge of top of Boyscout slab. Climb up, staying always right of the corner, to top.

37 CHIAROSCURO, F9B. Start at semi-corner 10 feet right of Brinton's Crack, directly below Hilton Ledge (see below). Climb face left of corner to Hilton Ledge, then directly up wall to top. Variation, F9A. Start from left side of Boyscout slab, climb thin crack up to Hilton Ledge.

38 BRINTON'S CRACK, F6. A classic climb, made worthwhile by a series of continuous exposed moves. It was first ascended in 1941, and its crux still embarrasses many climbers. Start in crack near corner of the buttress, beginning 20 feet up. (This point is reached by scrambling up slabby rock.) Climb the crack to one step below a rectangular niche (A), traverse delicately right to (or almost to) a platform (Hilton Ledge), then up jam crack to top. (A) BRINTON'S DIRECT, F8. Do not traverse, continue up near corner to top.

38A BRINTON'S CORNER, F10A. Climb corner all the way to top.

Brinton's Crack (route 38, diagram IV E)

61

39 BERKELEY, F6. Another classic. The easiest line on this wall starts at crack 20 feet left of corner of the buttress. Climb crack 20 feet and traverse right to ledge under first small overhang. Move up right, then climb somewhat left to exit crack leading into hanging chimney. This route can be varied considerably.

39A ROCOCO VARIATIONS, F7. Start near right corner, climb flake edge crack 30 feet to join regular Berkeley route.

40 CHICAGO, F8. One of the so-called hero climbs. The quality of the protection is unspeakably poor. Start same crack as Berkeley. Climb 25 feet to triangular niche (last protection until after crux), continue the crack up and left past long sustained crux, surmount final overhang just below top.

41 EVANSTON TOWNSHIP, F9A. Start from platform at base of Puff N' Grunt Chimney, climb thin crack parallel to Chicago.

42 PUFF N' GRUNT CHIMNEY, F6. Climb one of two inside corners to base of the chimney, then up chimney to top. Several wedged chockstones are useful. NOTE: there is a 4th-class access route in the broken area to the west.

43 THE RACK, F7. Dangling climbers are a common sight here. Start at crack curving right, capped by overhang. Follow crack to small platform on right corner, step up left (crux), climb corner blocks to a ledge, finish on wall right of the corner. Variation, F6. From small platform on right corner traverse right 10 feet and climb wall to same corner block as in The Rack.

44 THOROUGHFARE, F10A. Start at short inside corner 5 feet right of The Grotto. Climb the inside corner with use of adjacent (right) crack. Continue up thin cracks on the spectacular green wall above. Variation, F10B. Start on outside just right of the inside corner, climb directly up without using the inside corner or left crack above.

44A LUNAR ECLIPSE, F10A. Climb crack in right wall of The Grotto. Continue up over the middle of the right (higher) overhang.

45 THE GROTTO, F5. Start in dark chimney, climb past chockstones to platform on outside (top of chimney had been filled with rock). Finish by crack or inside corner above the platform. Variation, F5. Walk deeper into the chimney then climb up and out to the platform.

45A SOLAR ECLIPSE, F7. Climb left wall 4 feet inside The Grotto.

45B MOUSE TRAP, F10A. Face near corner.

46 VACILLATION, F7. Start at crack with bulge 10 feet up. Climb crack to a slightly loose hanging block, then up right to wide crack and to top.

47 MOUSE'S MISERY, F9B. Start on face just left of Vacillation, climb up left 25 feet to overhang, turn overhang at left crack, and follow crack to top. MOUSE TRACKS, F10B. Climb right side of the overhang into the appalling looking solution pockets above.

48 FULL STOP, F6. An old classic called "Two Pines." Start, thin crack leading to square niche. (Other slight cracks and holds 5-10 feet on left can also be used.) From the niche climb over elephant ear bulge (A), move 5 feet left and up to hanging gully with several pine trees, loose rock on ledge. Traverse right onto broken section of the wall and ascend. BIG DEAL, F9A. At (A) climb up thin crack about 5 feet left of Mouse's Misery.

49 THE REPRIEVE, F7. Start just right of corner, climb up (crux not high off ground) and left to a stance, continue up face, staying right of the corner.

50 SCHIZOPHRENIA, F6. Start below overhanging nose 25 feet up. Climb into dark pocket, continue around left side of the nose or directly over it, then up ridge above, finishing on corner left of the pine tree gully.

51 MODERATION, F4. Start up broken rock, traverse right above the nose on Schizophrenia, then up the easy ridge. Variation, F6. Start same but continue straight up groove that intersects the ridge higher up.

A rock and clay gully angles steeply left from the start of Moderation, an F4 route, to the top. It provides access to the next three climbs.

52 TOUCH AND GO, F7. Start halfway up the gully (small maple tree), at base of steep wall. Move up right then back left, following a set of small ledges to top of the crackless green wall.

53 DYSPEPSIA, F6. About halfway up this wall you'll wish for your pills. Start in gully as above, a little past the small tree. Climb crack on left side of the steep wall, ending just right of the dark overhang near top. PUSSY GALORE'S FLYING CIRCUS, F7. Start below flake (detached block) in line with the dark overhang. Climb edge of the flake and continue until below right side of the overhang. Instead of exiting right, traverse left on good footholds then up (crux) up.

54 JOLLY GENDARME, F5. Start in upper part of the gully from Moderation. Traverse left around the gendarme (on southwest side of the gully) to crack with pine tree, then climb the crack.

55 GERITOL, F10B. Start at base of wall with dirty yellow lichen. Climb on very small awkward holds until below hanging corner, then up right side of the corner. The wall between Geritol and Chlorosis has two cracks. Right crack, F9B, left crack, F10A.

64

The following three climbs (56, 57, and 58) start in same inside corner.

56 CHLOROSIS, F7. Climb inside corner to overhang 30 feet up. Step right and climb the overhang to crack above, follow crack to top.

57 HYPOGLYCEMIA, F7. Start from same inside corner, above the overhang on Chlorosis. Climb the overhanging crack and groove on right wall.

MANY PINES BUTTRESS to BILL'S BUTTRESS (Diagram V E)

58 ANEMIA, F4. Originally Many Pines. Start in same inside corner, climb to ledge with first pine tree on left, continue by one of the numerous variations from the ledge.

59 BROKEN LADDER, F7. Climb face up to the pine tree ledge. Several routes are possible. Route finding is the crux of this climb.

60 PETER'S PROJECT, F7. Start in overhanging crack, climb crack until the angle eases, then move fairly straight up face and cracks to top.

60A PETER'S PROJECT RIGHT SIDE, F9A. Climb the face about 5 feet right of Peter's Project. The crack is off limits.

61 OSTENTATION, F9A. Start below corner with overhang 10 feet up. Climb to the overhang, traverse left, then climb up right to good holds and continue corner to top.

62 CALLIPIGEANOUS CRACK, F9B. An exercise in muscle climbing. Climb (finger) jam crack onto loose block, exit right to corner. CALLIPIGEANOUS DIRECT, F10A. Continue straight up from the block.

63 MICHAEL'S PROJECT, F7. Start in prominent groove and crack, step right to easier holds 10-15

Diagram V E

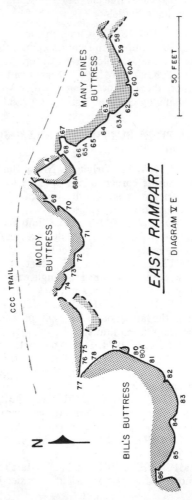

feet up, back into the crack until below overhang, exit right to large ledge from which there are a couple of ways to finish. KAMA-KAZI, F8. Climb, using inside corner crack only, directly up overhang to top.

63A NO TRUMP, F10B. This avoids holds in the crack. Start 3 feet right of Michael's Project, and stay within a few feet of the crack, ending on the exit ledge.

64 FLATUS, F10A. Easily identified by the lack of identifiable holds. Climb wall past two bolts approximately 20 and 25 feet up, left under overhang, and up. FLATUS DIRECT, F10B. Continue straight up over roof to wall and top.

65 THE BLACK RIB, F10A. Getting off the ground is the first crux. Start in pit below dark section of the wall, climb to the hanging chimney above.

65A DOUBLE CLUTCH, F10C. Start in pit. Climb face left of The Black Rib, not using holds on either route 65 or 66.

66 MAN AND SUPERMAN, F10A. Climb corner to top. Few supermen attempt this.

67 THE SEWING MACHINE, F6. An unusual climb for Devil's Lake. One's legs give out before one's arms, unless legs and arms give out together. Climb dirty flared chimney to top. Loose rock near top.

68 JAMBOREE, F6. Start in chimney (which gives an F4 access route behind the small tower), then jam up deep cracks on right wall. ALGAE, F5. Start left of the chimney, follow a crack up and right to a flake in the chimney. Variation, F9A. From top of crack climb left and up.

68A F5. Climb the tower starting near south corner.

69 LICHEN, F4. Climb behind one of the large flakes and continue up wall to top.

70 FUNGUS, F7. Climb face left of the flakes using crusty holds.

71 NINE-MINUS, F8. Start in shallow inside corner capped by overhang. Climb up, exiting right below the overhang, then up and left. TEN-MINUS, F9A. Climb the face right of the inside corner, then left as before. ELEVEN-MINUS, F9C. Continue directly up the (right) face. HALES CORNER, F10A. Climb corner 5 feet left of Nine-Minus.

72 CUL-DE-SAC, F8. A deceptive line, it is much harder than it looks. Start in inside corner capped by square overhang. Climb up and right (crux) past the overhang. Scramble up short chimney to a ledge and to top. MOTHER OF PEARL, F9B. Climb face only, on right side of the inside corner. CUL-DE-SAC EXIT, F10B. Mantel at roof, and continue up and left to top. FIBULA CRACKS, F10B. Start in shallow inside corner 5 feet left of Cul-de-sac. Climb straight up, at 35 feet pass an overhang on the right.

73 TIBIA CRACK, F8. Start in crack leading to hanging chimney between two overhangs. Climb crack, enter the chimney, and exit (usually) right.

74 HORTICULTURE, F5. There are large rotten overhangs high up on this line. The most interesting start is on the outside of a semi-attached pillar (or use crack on either side of the pillar). Climb pillar, then up into inside corner beneath the overhangs, exit right to top. ROOFUS, F8. Exit left from the overhangs. NOTE: left of Horticulture there is an access route (4th class) on grassy ledges (avoid the chimney with loose rock).

75 DOG LEG, F5. Start in dirt gully (near base of The Dark Corner). Climb groove that first angles right then goes straight up. Continue on ledges to top.

76 PROPHET'S HONOR, F9A. Start in gully as above, climb overhanging wall to right of The Dark Corner.

77 THE DARK CORNER, F5. A dark, stygian chimney.

78 BREAKFAST OF CHAMPIONS, F7. Climb long jam crack ending on huge flake, then up left to top.

79 IGNOMINY, F5. Start near corner, climb broken crack up and right onto northeast wall of the buttress (white rock), up wall 10 feet (crux), continue up ledges into inside corner with pine tree, then to top.

80 THE CHEATAH, F9B. An exceptionally continuous route. Climb long crack which ends with a difficult layback near right corner. (The last moves can be avoided.)

80A PUSSY CAT, F10B. Climb the wall left of The Cheatah, stay 4 feet left of crack to top. **TOM CAT, F10C.** A very difficult start. Start just left of Pussy Cat, climb left and up staying between routes 80A and 81 on good holds.

81 PUSH-MI PULL-YU, F6. An old classic called "Three Pines." A popular route with excellent protection. Climb (several ways) to crack beginning 20 feet up with pine tree above. Climb crack to the pine, scramble up ledges to top.

82 AGNOSTIC, F7. Climb into prominent alcove, step left onto ledge, up face and thin crack directly above the alcove, passing left of pine tree.

83 GRAND INQUISITOR, F7. An indistinct line that prohibits traversing to the easier climbs on either side. Start at lowest point of Bill's Buttress. Climb 10 feet to ledge, then up (slightly left) 15 feet into shallow groove or trough (obscure from the ground). Continue on easier rock to overhanging layback crack, up crack ending on small tower.

84 COATIMUNDI CRACK, F6. Start in prominent groove and crack. Climb the crack past overhanging section and step right onto ledge, then up to base of corner (small tower above). Continue up near the corner or step left to ledge and stem up inside corner (V-chimney) ending behind the tower. OVEREXTENSION, F6. Exit left from the groove, angling up to first ledge on Escalation.

85 ESCALATION, F6. Climb crack 20 feet (crux) to ledge and pine tree (A), then to another ledge and pine tree, and to top. Variation, F6. From ledge (A) traverse right on a narrow exposed ledge, join either of the two preceding routes. Variation, F9A. From left side of ledge (A) climb narrow southwest face, finish on lichen-covered narrow buttress.

86 THE OUTHOUSE, F7. Start under overhang between the two buttresses. Climb either side of the overhang, pass next overhang (a huge wedged block) also on either side.

RAINY WEDNESDAY TOWER to LEANING TOWER GULLY (Diagram VI E)

87 FALSE ALARM JAM, F6. The southeast side of Rainy Wednesday Tower. Start on broken rock to obvious crack in red rock, climb crack to a ledge, climb up either side of a slab boulder, continue on southeast face to top of the tower. Descent route: Climb down short chimney on northeast side, then jump off behind the tower. Continue down chimney west of the tower to base of cliff. Loose rock in gully above chimney.

88 RESURRECTION, F9A. Start on a large block at base of smooth face (pointed ceiling above). Climb face near right edge until able to move left and up into bowl-shaped area. Continue up to the ceiling and exit right. Variation, A2, F7. Nail up center of the smooth face, step left (free) and up into bowl as above.

A LAUNDRY CHUTE, F10B. Climb left side of face past two smaller overhangs. Continue up and under right side of large overhang. Climb hanging chute in overhang. Variation, NO STARCH, F10B. To avoid chute pass overhang on right.

9 EAVE OF DESTRUCTION, F9A. Start same as Double Overhang until under the ceiling, step right (fixed pin) and up. Variation, F7. Step right about 15 feet below the ceiling then up corner.

90 DOUBLE OVERHANG, F5. A well-protected route sufficiently exposed to maintain interest. Start in inside corner below ceiling. Climb crack in the corner, exit left and up to a platform. Climb right onto "lemon squeezer" block (A) then up into recess beneath right side of upper overhang. (If you climb directly up from the platform toward the overhang it is necessary to step right around a rib to attain this recess.) Step left and up into notch in the overhang, continue to top of the tower. Variation, F7. At (A) traverse right 10 feet and step around corner into groove and climb to top.

90A F5. Climb face directly to the platform.

90B OUT OF THE WOODS, F8. Climb southeast face.

91 BIRNAM WOOD, F7. Crack hidden and jealousy guarded by a tree. Variation, F10B. Cracks and overhang 4-6 feet left of Birnam Wood. Climb slabs to first crack (25 feet up), move left to pass overhang, climb right and follow thin cracks to top.

92 THE GREEN BULGE, F7. Start at prominent red slab. Climb slab (various routes) to base of green bulge, up bulge (from left or right) to a ledge, continue up (crux shortly above the ledge), ending just right of small tower.

Diagram VI E

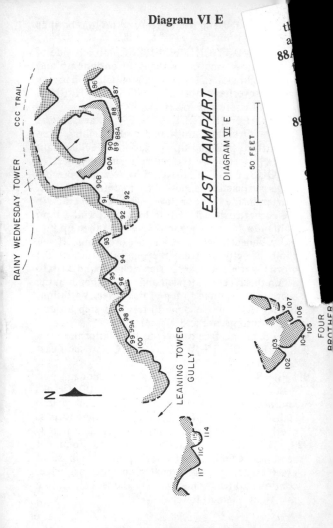

EAST RAMPART

DIAGRAM VI E

50 FEET

71

93 THE BALCONY, F5. Climb the inside corner, passing band of fairly unconsolidated rock.

94 THE MEZZANINE, F5. Start on outside of minor buttress that reaches halfway up the wall. Climb the buttress to base of groove (inside corner), then climb groove to top.

95 SECOND BALCONY, F5. Another inside corner or chimney, same description as The Balcony.

96 HIRSUTE, F7. Climb face and two overhangs directly.

97 CEREBRATION, F5. Inside corner with overhang near top. Pass overhang on right. Variation, F5. Start at short jam crack to right of the inside corner, then up broken rock.

98 SECOND COMING, F7. Start at base of steep face. Climb layback "crack" 20 feet to ledge on right, continue up until it is possible to traverse left and up to top. Variation, F9A. Start 4 feet left of Cerebration. Climb straight up and join Second Coming at 20-foot ledge.

99 ORGASM, F8. Try not to become overly excited by this intimidating line. Start, inside corner below large ceiling. Climb to smooth wall on right side of the inside corner, mantel up, step right around corner and on to top.

99A ORGASM DIRECT, F10A. Start 4 feet right of corner to top.

100 FOREPLAY, F6. Climb crack to pine tree, step right and climb into inside corner to left of the ceiling on Orgasm, then up past overhang to top. Watch for loose rock on top.

101 THE FRICTION SLAB (not on diagram) is one of several boulder problems below Orgasm. Both right and left sides of the slab have been ascended "no hands."

FOUR BROTHERS (Diagram VI E)

102 FAMILY JEWELS, F7. Start from pedestal left of corner, step right around the corner to hidden dihedral, climb the dihedral, then a short jam crack finishes it.

103 GRAVEL PIT, F5. Climb the inside corner, laybacking past overhang into the gravel.

104 FOLIAGE, F5. Follow crack up and left across the face.

105 ZOT, F7. Start at same crack as Foliage, step onto right corner, then climb the corner.

106 CATALEPSY, F6. Start in crack using chimney technique on face to the right, climb into prominent groove above.

107 DECADENCE, F5. Follow this grungy crack up to overhanging block, exit left when your belayer isn't looking.

LEANING TOWER (Diagram VII E)

108 SOUTH FACE, F4. Climb center or either corner of the face.

109 WEST FACE, F8. Start from right edge, climb the smooth face without using prominent holds (specifically the triangular niche) on left. Variation, F4. Start at left corner (above low platform), climb up and right to top.

110 NORTHWEST FACE, F7. Start at center of this narrow face, climb up and right.

111 NORTH FACE, F10A. Start at center of the smooth overhanging face, climb up to small pocket, up left to another pocket, then to top.

112 EAST FACE, F7. Start from right edge, up left to top of the overhanging wall. Variation, F7. Start from left edge of the face.

113 THE TOMBSTONE is across the trail from Leaning Tower. Many variations on the short walls are possible, some very difficult.

Diagram VII E

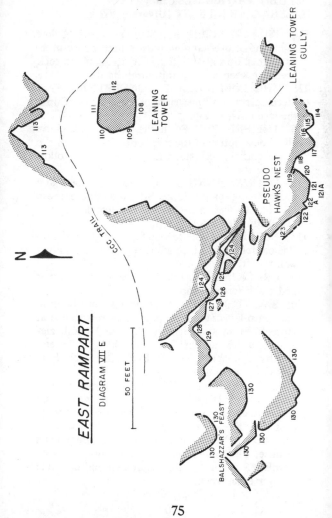

EAST RAMPART

DIAGRAM VII E

50 FEET

N

CCC TRAIL

LEANING TOWER

LEANING TOWER GULLY

PSEUDO HAWKS NEST

BALSHAZZAR'S FEAST

75

114 WILD HORSES, F8. Start at corner below right side of overhanging nose. Climb above overhang, then up slab or left corner. Erosion and rock breakage keep making this climb harder.

115 THE IMMACULATE CONCEPTION, F9A. Steep narrow wall just right of The Pretzel. Climb the face only, to top.

116 THE PRETZEL, F6. Is the name of this climb also a description of the climber on it? Start in the inside corner, very steep for 15 feet, then follow crack to top.

117 DRUNKEN SAILOR, F6. Many climbers lose their bearings on this route. Start left of nose, move up right 15 feet to a stance, then wander up the broad rounded ridge to top.

118 EPIPHANY, F8. Start on face to right of the inside corner. Climb face along a crack, eliminating wall to left.

119 CRACKING UP, F6. Prominent inside corner and crack (crux at top).

120 BAGATELLE, F10C. Climb mini-overhang to crack, up left of crack to temporary rest stance at 20 feet. From stance move right and climb zigzagging up to and past 8-inch overhang at 35 feet. Climb ridge above to top. PHLOGISTON, F11. Left crack in same wall.

121 BEGINNER'S DEMISE, F10A. Start at base of steep wall just left of corner, climb wall near or on corner to easier rock above. Difficult bulge can be passed by a few unusual moves to easier rock.

121A ABM, F10A. Often mistaken for Beginner's Demise. The route runs 4-6 feet left of Beginner's Demise. Start on short difficult wall and continue up over easier rock.

122 BEGINNER'S DELIGHT, F5. An aptly named climb. Several variations are possible at the start. Climb 30 feet to detached block, traverse right to corner at this level or climb crack to below overhanging block, then traverse, climb corner to top.

122A CHICKEN DELIGHT, F7. Start just right of sharp narrow rib, climb layback crack 15 feet, continue straight up past overhanging block (35 feet) to top. Variation, F8. Stay to left of Chicken Delight up steep hard crack.

123 HERO'S FRIGHT, F7. A crack is visible near upper left corner of the wall. Climb lower wall to base of the crack, follow crack to top.

124 DEATH AND TRANSFIGURATION, F5. Climb (any way) onto large narrow blocks detached from the wall, step into prominent dihedral, climb past black bulge of loose rock to a broad ledge. Walk off right or finish in crack 20 feet left. Variation, F8. Start on right block (near auxiliary access gully), climb bulging wall above.

125 DEATH AND DISFIGURATION, F8. Start on left detached block, climb thin crack to the broad ledge.

126 PRIME RIB, F9A. Ascend the rib until it fades out (at the level of the overhang on Bloody Mary), then up slightly left past small niche to the broad ledge.

127 BLOODY MARY, F8. Look for large bulge of loose rock with a meaty crack through the center. Start in groove directly below the bulge, climb the groove, surmount the overhang by hand jams and face holds to an awkward stance, then up left to ledge left of prominent upper corner. Finish on wall above the ledge. THE FAKIR, F7. Start same point, climb left crack 20 feet to a platform, traverse up and right to the awkward stance.

128 OCTOBER FIRST, F7. Inside corner, a strenuous layback that degenerates after the first few moves.

129 ANCHOR'S AWAY, F8. Steep short wall. Climb crack behind either pine tree. (Left crack is F6.)

130 BALSHAZZAR'S FEAST, F5-F7. A veritable feast of climbing, in three courses. There are many variations, especially on the lowest wall.

HAWK'S NEST (Diagram VIII E)

131 HAPPY HUNTING GROUNDS, F10A. Climb thin steep crack, continue to ceiling high on the wall, climb out over right side to top. Leaders who fall on this climb may go to the Happy Hunting Grounds. FLAKES AWAY, F10A. Climb wall 4-5 feet left of Happy Hunting Grounds.

131A R. EXAM, F9B. Climb following black water marks. Pass small 8-inch overhang on right.

131B DOUBLE HERNIA, F10A. Climb following thin crack to ledge at 20 feet. Continue on right of (avoiding) corner.

132 BUCKET BRIGADE, F6. Start in The Funnel, a cleft or groove 25 feet high, to broken rock and bushes. (Here two main variations branch out. Bucket Brigade is the more easterly alternative.) Continue almost straight up for 30 feet to ledge (A) at base of prominent inside corner. Climb the inside corner past overhang to top. HALLUCINATION, F5. At (A) step right to outside ledge, then up and left to exit crack in wall above.

133 THE RAMP, F6. Start as above. From top of The Funnel climb left wall 15 feet to base of lower angle slab. Climb either side of the slab, then up to broad ledge (B). (The ledge system west of this point is commonly used to traverse off the wall.) Climb the obvious chimney at the east end of the

Diagram VIII E

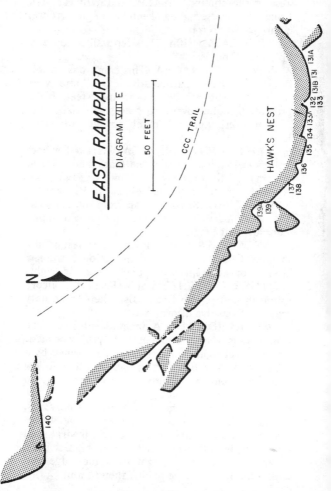

EAST RAMPART

DIAGRAM VIII E

50 FEET

CCC TRAIL

N

HAWK'S NEST

131A
131
131B
132
133
133A
134
135
136
137
138
139
139A
140

79

ledge or climb the wall at one of several points west of the chimney. WALPURGISNACHT, F6. From (B) traverse right and enter a hanging groove, climb groove to top.

133A PIEPLATE, F10A. Up steep wall to top over "pie plate" holds.

134 VIVISECTION, F10A. This climb has an unforgettable start, particularly if you lose your fingers on it. Start beneath overhang 5 feet off the ground. Conquer overhang onto small slab, pass smaller overhang, then climb straight up steep ledges.

135 ALPHA CENTAURI, F10A. Start a few feet left of Vivisection, a disjointed crack and layback system (slightly overhanging). Climb 10 feet (crux), continue up the steep ledges as in Vivisection. YELLOW PAGES, F10A. Start from top of block. Let your fingers do the walking and join Alpha Centauri at 12 feet.

136 ANOMIE, F8. Climb into alcove 15 feet off the ground. Climb out to the right, follow a shallow trough or concavity that angles slightly right. MOTHER FLETCHER'S, F8. From the alcove climb up left to join Charybdis. There is no easy way out from this alcove.

137 CHARYBDIS, F7. A magnificent line. The climbing is very continuous but well protected. Start 15 feet right of the inside corner formed by a large block. Climb 15 feet straight up, then follow thin crack angling slightly right, continue up to the exit ledge and to top.

138 SCYLLA, F7. Climb 15 feet as in Charybdis, continue slightly left to a comfortable ledge 30 feet up. Climb into dark overhang or dihedral that rises steeply to the right, follow it to highest overhanging point (or step right from the ledge and climb the face to same point), then to top.

139 CORONARY, F7. Start on the large block at west end of the wall. (You can walk or climb up to this point.) Move up and right, mantling onto a ledge (same as on Scylla). Step left and up to a possibly loose block between two prominent overhangs, then up the shallow (right) groove, which is well supplied with fixed pins. There is a left groove accessible by stepping left from the loose block. ANGINA, F9B. Start same block, climb up toward the overhang above, exit right and directly up into left groove of Coronary.

139A ANGINA II, F9B. Climb past Angina overhang, on left, into hanging inside corner with old piton.

140 LAND'S END, F7. The rock immediately west of Hawk's Nest is rather shattered. There is a more challenging route on a buttress 150 feet northwest of Hawk's Nest. Climb the steep south face and overhang.

Doorway Rocks

The Doorway Massif is perhaps the most expansive cliff area at Devil's Lake. When seen from the campground at the south end of the lake its 200-foot height captures the eye and staggers the imagination. Despite first appearance, the area is quite broken up. The tallest vertical walls are about 60 feet. The unique feature of the area is the possibility of multiple pitch climbing, with mountain-type scrambling and route finding. A large gully divides the Massif into the MAJOR MASS and MINOR MASS. The larger (westerly) Major Mass, which includes the distinctive DEVIL'S DOORWAY formation, is further divided into an Upper Band and a Lower Band. The two bands are separated by a terrace and ledge system that in places contains a 20-foot middle band of rocks. Recommended climbs in the Major Mass: Angel's Crack, F6; Mary Jane, F8; Keyhole Chimney, F5; King's Corner, F6; Dippy Diagonal, F6; Red Slab, F5; TM Overhang, F9A; Jungle Gym, F5; The Playground, F6.

The Minor Mass consists mainly of a single large buttress with two distinct levels. The lower (south) level reaches a high point designated the SOUTH TOWER. The saddle behind the South Tower is accessible by a short climb from either side. Routes: Pigeon Roof, F6; B-Minor Mass, F5; Green Ledges, F7.

The RED ROCKS (sometimes called the Gorge or Devil's Alley) is along the Potholes Trail, east of the Doorway Rocks. This accessible area is often used for beginner groups, though being right on a hiking trail is an unfavorable feature.

There are many small rocks immediately west of the main Doorway Massif; these are described briefly under RAMSEY'S PINNACLE.

Approaches to the Doorway Rocks: Hike up the talus slope to the base of the Lower Band. Or hike partway up the Potholes Trail and cut 100 yards west to the base of the Minor Mass and The Keyhole. When approaching from above, use the short scenic trail that dips down from the summit trail, giving access to Devil's Doorway and the top of the Upper Band. Then descend the gully between the Major Mass and Minor Mass, or a broken section west of the Major Mass, to reach the lower level.

MAJOR MASS, Upper Band (Diagrams IX E, X E)

DEVIL'S DOORWAY has several interesting climbs on its twin pillars. It is the scene of many dramatic demonstrations of rock climbing techniques to the passing tourists. An eye bolt on top is useful as a belay and rappel anchor. The northwest corner (1) or chimney (3) are usually used to ascend to set upper belays.

1 ROMPER, F4. Climb ledges at northwest corner of the formation. There is one perplexing move near the top.

2 LAZY DAY, F7. Climb north face near left edge.

3 DOORWAY CHIMNEY, F4. The chimney walls have been worn smooth by the boots and butts of many climbers. Those with long legs may feel unpleasantly cramped.

4 IMPOSSIBLE CRACK, F7. Start from inside the Doorway, climb left into the crack (half the battle), then jam or layback to top. Variation, F8. Start on wall below the crack, climb up, passing overhang into the crack.

5 UP YOURS TOO, F8. Climb south end of the south pillar.

6 BLOODY FINGER, F6. Climb southwest side of the south pillar. A fall from this knife-edge crack can be messy.

7 F6. Climb southwest side of the north pillar.

UPPER BAND. Several gullies can be used to descend from the trail to the base of the Upper Band. Probably the most convenient is reached at route 17.

8 F6. Crack.

9 F4. Crack.

10 THE THREE KINGS, F7. Three large blocks form a ridge at the east end of the Upper Band. Climb the short strenuous layback between the west and middle Kings.

11 Deleted.

12-16 This small buttress has several short routes. The MAGICAL MYSTERY TOUR is for beginners: Start at low point near south corner (14),

Diagram IX E

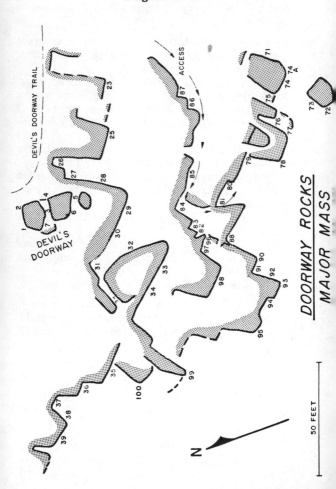

Diagram X E

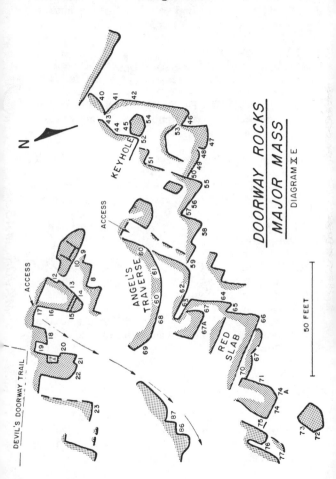

DOORWAY ROCKS
MAJOR MASS

DIAGRAM X E

50 FEET

climb southeast side to base of huge detached block, traverse around south end of the buttress onto slanty ledge (15), climb up behind the detached block and scramble to top.

17 F3. Access route.

18 HIDDEN WALL, F8. The headwall between two more prominent buttresses. Climb the face and overhang.

19 THE CRYPT, F4. Is it actually possible to escape from this rock tomb? Start in gully below, climb a narrow chimney past chockstone into the crypt.

19A F5. From base of The Crypt traverse left into an open alcove and stem to top.

20 FAITH, HOPE AND CHARITY, F5. Start from bottom of east face, follow crack past small overhang.

21 ANGEL'S CRACK, F6. A dihedral marked by a steep arrowhead slab. Climb past the slab, exit right to top.

22 THE JOLLY ROGER, F8. Climb the southwest face, following crack system past two small niches.

23 F5. Crack and corner.

24 Deleted.

25 MARY JANE, F8. Climb right side of south face to last ledge, then (crux) step onto toehold at right corner and reach for finger jam. Variation, F6. Start as above, traverse left to good ledge at west corner, mantel to top.

26 F4. Chockstone chimney. (Possible access route.)

27 F6. Crack.

28 INDECISION, F5. Climb cracked face, ending below blocks at south end of Devil's Doorway. Two distinct lines are possible, but most climbers zigzag, finding the easiest route.

29 CEDAR TREE WALL, F5. There are two crack climbs on this wall. Start behind cedar tree to reach right crack, climb crack past pine tree to top. The left crack ends short of the top; complete the route by climbing a short wall.

30 CANNABIS SATIVA, F8. Short face climb. Start on small holds and end with crack.

JUNGLE GYM TOWER (routes 32-34) stands out slightly from the wall behind it. The narrow gap separating the tower can be crossed by jumping. To reach the climbs from above, descend the gully **(31)** on the east side of the tower. Most often the tower is ascended as part of a multiple pitch route starting on the Lower Band (see Seventh Buttress).

32 F5. Climb east face of Jungle Gym Tower from the gully.

33 JUNGLE GYM, F5. Start on top of the Seventh Buttress of the Lower Band, up jam crack to a ledge, then up to a sloping platform customarily used to belay. Mantel up on west side of the platform and climb to top of the tower. Variation, F5. From the belay platform traverse to the crack (32) of the east face.

34 JUNGLE GYM CHIMNEY, F5. Start on top of Seventh Buttress as above, but farther left, below pine tree. Climb 15 feet, then traverse left across a slab using flake handholds, continue up chimney behind west side of Jungle Gym Tower.

35 THE PLAYGROUND, F6. Don't forget to look over there! A not-too-steep face for practice on small hold technique. If you begin at the bottom, where the face is narrow, there is an initial serious move. Thereafter there is a choice of routes, easier right and harder left.

36-39 Short climbs.

MAJOR MASS, Lower Band (Diagrams IX E, X E)

THE KEYHOLE (routes 40-54) is the easternmost buttress of the Lower Band. Most of the climbs cross one of two platforms on the north and south sides of The Keyhole.

40   SUNKEN SLAB, F6. Start at recessed section well up (north) along the base of the buttress. Climb the approximate center of lower slab to overhang, step up onto lip of the overhang and follow a slight hollow in upper slab to a stance. Traverse left (south) on wafer footholds to join 44 or climb short jam crack beneath highest overhang and exit left.

NOTE: The Sunken Slab provides an F4 access to North Platform on left.

41   PROSPERITY, F5. Begin in the crack just left of the Sunken Slab, angle left following good holds up the outside corner.

42   HAMMER CRACK, F8. There is a tradition (best forgotten) of using a wedged piton hammer to aid this climb. Climb crack straight up from bottom to North Platform. Variation, F6. Traverse from right into the crack 5 feet up.

43-45   NORTH PLATFORM continuations.

43   F5. At north edge of the platform climb up and right above the Sunken Slab.

44   F7. Start in a slabby groove, climb to overhanging crack (crux) that leads into an inside corner.

45   TOP SHELF, F7. Start on face just left of The Keyhole, up face to an underhold, then left and up to ledge under a roof, traverse left, escaping the roof onto a sloping shoulder, continue up southeast ridge above The Keyhole.

NOTE: The Keyhole chimney is accessible directly from the North Platform or by traversing around to the south side; see climb 52.

46 STETTNER'S OVERHANG, F6. Start below right side of an awesome ceiling. Use holds to right of the deep crack (staying in the crack is harder), climb past the ceiling, then follow the crack over a mild overhang to the South Platform.

47 F4. An easy but exposed face route to the South Platform. This has an interesting F6 variation if you traverse right just above the overhang then up the face or right corner.

48 EASY STREET, F3. The easiest route to the South Platform. Climb the obvious block-filled chimney.

49 F6. Thin crack.

50 HARD TIMES, F5. Inside corner with small overhang 20 feet up.

51-54 SOUTH PLATFORM continuations. From the South Platform it is possible to exit northwest through a broken area until the ledge system separating the Lower and Upper Bands is reached.

51 F5. Inside corner leading onto slab at top of Keyhole Buttress.

52 KEYHOLE CHIMNEY, F5. Scramble up ledges to base of The Keyhole. Move up the crack to reach "thank God" hold and swing into the chimney; alternatively, traverse a ledge (54) around outside of the Keyhole Pillar and enter chimney from the north. Exit from chimney onto south face to top of the buttress, or move up awkwardly high inside The Keyhole and exit northeast.

53 F5. Climb mostly broken rock above east end of the South Platform to ledge (54) above. It is interesting to traverse right onto the steep east face and climb past a small pine tree to reach the same ledge.

54 NONCONFORMIST, F7. Start on ledge level with base of The Keyhole, climb southeast face of Keyhole Pillar.

55 KING'S CORNER, F6. The corner is not climbed directly from the bottom; instead start from right inside corner (50) and traverse onto the corner 12 feet up. (Same point can be reached from left on first ledge of Dippy Diagonal, but the traverse here is F8.) Up corner past overhang, step right to hanging crack in east face (can be avoided by staying left of corner), up crack, then regain corner and follow it to top of crowning pinnacle.

56 DIPPY DIAGONAL, F6. Climb the crack that diagonals slightly left. Variation, F8. Start on first ledge (15 feet up), to the right of Dippy Diagonal. Climb face and thin crack, through a niche, ending on next large ledge.

57 KENOSIS, F5. Climb crack and inside corner to second large ledge (pine tree), then up between awkward blocks above the inside corner. From here climb a small tower on the left, or go west to a couloir (59) to reach Angel's Traverse.

58 F5. Minor broken buttress left of Kenosis has one or two interesting points.

59 F4. Access couloir.

60 ANGEL'S TRAVERSE, F5. An exposed ledge spanning the upper mass of a high rounded buttress. The ledge is ordinarily used for walking on. Start traversing from head of access couloir (59), or start lower in the couloir and climb a short crack to reach the traverse ledge. At the far (west) end of the traverse climb a chimney 20 feet to top of the buttress. There are two other ascent routes (from traverse ledge to top) on the south and southeast sides of the buttress; the more interesting one (61, F7) starts at the middle of the traverse.

62 F8. Start on short ledge 30 feet below Angel's Traverse (the ledge is reached easily from left chimney, 63). Climb crack up to west end of Angel's Traverse, crux just below small tree. Variation, F7. Start same point, climb diagonally right until a holdless section forces you farther right toward the access couloir (59).

63 F4. Chimney.

64 INNOCENCE, F7. The steep east face of the Red Slab Buttress. Start near dihedral (65), climb 15 feet, move right, then up center of face (crux) to slabbier rock above.

65 F5. Climb dihedral or adjacent crack to top of the Red Slab.

66 F5. Start at lowest point below southeast corner of the buttress, climb left onto a pedestal, step right back to the corner and up the Red Slab.

67 RED SLAB, F5. Climb the slightly overhanging system of good holds, continue up the Red Slab, perhaps belaying on top. Go around corner to right, climb the exposed southeast corner, with an interesting step-up on a licheny slab just below top of the buttress. Or finish on southwest side **(67A)**, doing a mantel and balance step to reach top. A humpy wall **(68)** behind top of the buttress provides a short continuation.

69 F9A. A short face (boulder problem).

70 CHOCKSTONE CHIMNEY, F5. You can raise the standard of this route by starting in the inside corner, otherwise simply walk up from the right on ledges. Stem past the large chockstone into the chimney above.

71 TM OVERHANG, F9A. Climb the tough layback crack on the east face to a resting place just below the overhang. Reach out for good holds above the overhang, then merely pull yourself up until footholds are found. Variation, F8. It is possible to exit left of the overhang.

72 LAYBACK BOULDER, F6. This is a large rock that impedes travel along the base of the Lower Band. Start on southwest side, swing right onto south slab, then climb the layback. Descend on the northeast side of the boulder.

73 F5. Short jam crack.

74 ARCHWAY COOKIE, F8. Start on southwest face above the Layback Boulder. Climb past bulge using friction handhold, move up under the arching overhang, traverse right around the arch, then climb to top of the buttress.

74A F6. Start on slabby rock at southeast corner of the buttress, climb onto a shelf above first overhang, traverse left onto southwest face, and continue as above.

75 F4. Descent route from the Archway Buttress; inexperienced climbers should use discretion.

77 BLUE SLAB, F5. Start at southeast corner (pine tree on first ledge), ascend the giant staircase to the Blue Slab at the top.

78 F5. Start at west corner, climb up and right more or less as above, or (F6) climb left into a wide angling crack on the west face. There are chimney routes **(76, 79)** on both sides of the Blue Slab Buttress.

80 F5. Inside corner crack.

81 ACCESS GULLY to top of the Lower Band. Start from the little inside corner, climb into the dirt gully then up and right to top of the band. There are several grimy climbs on the walls of the gully **(82-85)**; the best is route 84, an inside corner and chockstone crack.

86-87 F5-F4. Inside corners.

88 CAT WALK, F7. Start in the inside corner, climb up and traverse left stealthily on an irregular ledge, then up near left corner.

89 Deleted.

90-95 SEVENTH BUTTRESS of the Lower Band. This is the last or westernmost buttress under the former numbering system. It is the start of a popular 4 pitch route that includes Jungle Gym Tower above. The bottom section is broken with many closely spaced variations. The second pitch is usually one of the routes on the east side (96 or 97).

96 F4. Narrow corner or rib.

97 F7. Inside corner (an unpleasant layback) or adjacent crack that leads into the inside corner.

98 NO REST FOR THE WICKED, F8. Start just left of pine tree, climb the southwest face past three triangular pockets.

99 RIGHT ON, F5. A narrow, tall buttress or ridge, rather less than vertical. Start at inconspicuous point behind oak tree, climb past overhang, finish on either corner of the more prominent upper section.

100 F7. Corner 10 feet left of upper section of Right On.

RAMSEY'S PINNACLE (no diagram)

This is an area west of Devil's Doorway that has many low walls and towers. The pinnacle itself is 150 feet west of the Doorway. It has two routes that start together on the left side of the south face. One route goes straight up a slightly disconcerting groove (F6), the other angles right to a large chockstone at the top (F5).

The wall below Ramsey's Pinnacle has a wide variety of short climbs. Perhaps the most noteworthy route goes up an inside corner that ends on the platform at the base of Ramsey's Pinnacle.

Seventy-five feet southwest of the aforementioned

wall, across a gully that transects the entire area, there is a tower with steep southeast and southwest faces. Both faces are F9, the southeast face a particularly delicate route. A leadable F7 variation starts on the southeast face, then goes up just around the south (right) corner.

There are many other little climbs around, none of which is of great consequence. However, you may find it pleasant to explore, following the various terraces and gullies that give the area a rock garden character.

MINOR MASS (Diagram XI E)

1-5 East Buttress of the Minor Mass. This small formation is separated from the main buttress by a grungy gully. There are several ways to start, e.g., the southwest slab (4). Several ledges will be encountered, suggesting two or three pitches, but one long pitch will get you to the top. The upper pitch has an interesting variation on the east side (5).

6 Deleted.

7 OBDURACY, F6. Start right of oak tree, climb short wall to ledge above.

8 DISINCLINATION, F5. Start on ledge left of the grungy gully, climb to large pine tree and up the inclined chute behind the tree. Variation, F6. Climb overhanging blocks to right of the tree.

9 LADYFINGERS, F9A. Start on ledge as above, at base of steep wall behind pine tree. Climb the wall into a shallow groove, up groove to top.

10 PIGEON ROOF, F6. Climb crack leading to a prominent roof, pass the roof easily into the wide crack above. This crack is that perplexing in-between size—too small to chimney and too large to jam. Variation, F8. Traverse left underneath the roof, continue to top.

Diagram XI E

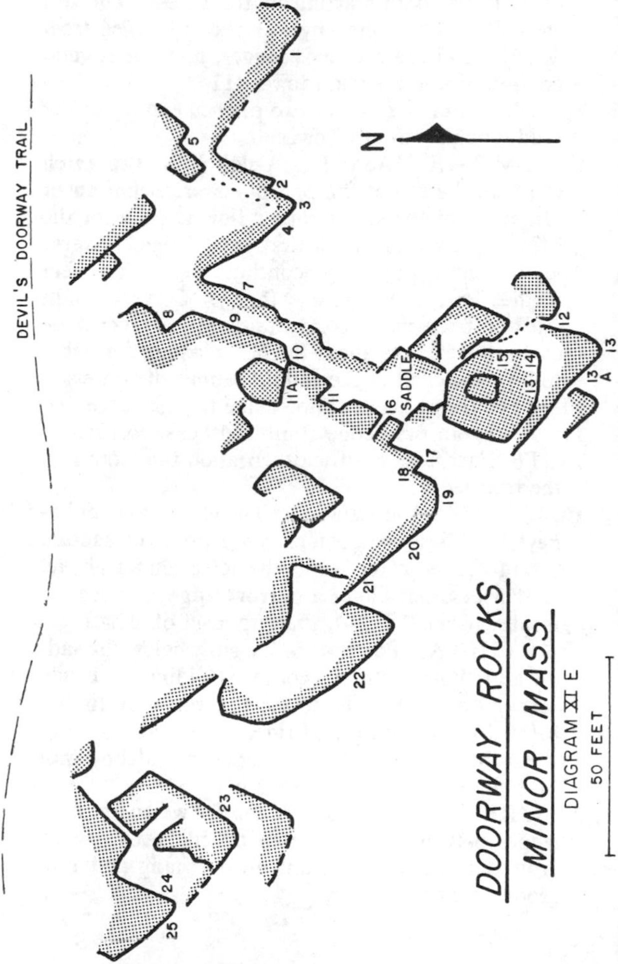

DEVIL'S DOORWAY TRAIL

N

DOORWAY ROCKS
MINOR MASS

DIAGRAM XI E

50 FEET

SADDLE

11 FLOTSAM AND JETSAM, F5. This is actually two climbs, both starting in the recess. The left chimney is obstructed by a partially toppled tree. The right inside corner is longer, and has a good continuation on a small tower **(11A)**.

12 F4. Chimney route in two pitches ending in the saddle behind South Tower.

13 B-MINOR MASS, F5. A delightful two pitch climb to the top of the South Tower. Begin on or just right of the south corner (lowest point of the Minor Mass). Climb to first good ledge, traverse left to small overhang, continue here, or 5 feet farther left, to next ledge (belay). Traverse right and climb the inside corner (alternatively, continue on southwest face above the belay ledge), scramble to top. Descend to the saddle behind the tower.

13A F6. Climb on southwest side to first ledge.

14 F7. From first ledge climb southeast corner.

15 F8. East face, a difficult variation that starts on the first ledge.

16, 18 Saddle continuations. The chockstone chimney (16, F5) is the obvious route from the saddle, giving access to (or from) the scree ledges above. Or traverse left along a narrow ledge into second inside corner (18, F4), then up a set of ledges.

17 Á CHEVAL, F6. Start in the gully below the saddle and climb the sharp corner, avoiding the inside corner on the left. Near the top you may find it helpful to mount up and ride.

19 F7. Start on rounded corner, climb slabby wall past right end of upper overhang.

20 GREEN LEDGES, F7. Climb the wall with three ledges 8-10 feet apart. From the highest ledge go around right corner, climb to overhang and into groove above.

Diagram XII E

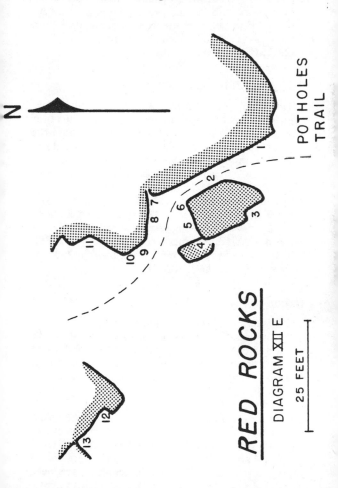

RED ROCKS

DIAGRAM XII E

25 FEET

21 MANHANDLER, F9A. Start 5 feet right of the inside corner, below a formidable overhang. Move up and right under the overhang, surmount it into the crack containing small birch tree.

22-25 Miscellaneous climbs.

RED ROCKS (Diagram XII E)

This small area is along the Potholes Trail, where the trail passes between a tower and a wall. The tower is usually ascended by stemming in the cleft above the trail (route **2**) or by the southwest dihedral (route **3**, F5). Once on top there is an easy descent at **4**, but it is more fun to lean across and then step over to the wall opposite the tower. There are other good beginner climbs on these rocks, e.g., route **7** (chimney) and route **9** (ledge/jam crack). For a more challenging climb try the overhanging section left of the chimney (route **8**, F9A), or a corner farther left (route **10**, F8). NOTE: There are a few more climbs within 200 feet on either side of the Red Rocks.

Balanced Rock Area

The section of the East Bluff considered here is more or less directly above the campground at the south end of Devil's Lake. Balanced Rock is located at the corner or ridge (facing southwest) that is formed by the right-angle bend in the bluff. Access is by Balanced Rock Trail, which starts just across the railroad tracks from the south campground. There is a traditional 15-foot practice rock on the trail, partway up the lower bluff boulderfield. The main climbing interest is centered on BALANCED ROCK WALL, halfway up the bluff. A large number of routes, a few up to 60 feet in length, have been worked out on this steep wall. A drawback to climbing here is the generally heavy trail traffic along the base of the wall. BOX CANYON is an alcove behind the east end of Balanced Rock Wall; it has some entertaining little climbs. There are other scattered climbing rocks on the upper half of the bluff, mostly to the east of Balanced Rock; a few of these are noted below. Recommended climbs: Watermarks, F8; Der Glotz, F9A; Sunken Pillar, F6.

BALANCED ROCK WALL (Diagram XIII E)

1 Deleted.
2 BASSWOOD CHIMNEY, F4. A bit awkward until a ledge (A) 20 feet up is reached, thereafter quite easy. Variation, F6. Climb to (A) as above, then climb a crack 5 feet right of the chimney.
3 MORNING AFTER, F10A. Start at left edge of the basswood thicket, climb the face to reach a bucket hold 20 feet up.
4 WATERMARKS, F8. The classic climb of the area. It appears on the "must" list of every aspiring climber. Start where the trail (from below) joins Balanced Rock Wall. Up 10 feet to a ledge (A), right to a crack with two triangular pocket holds, climb crack past bulge (crux) and continue to top. WATERMARKS DIRECT, F9C. Start directly below the triangular pockets, climb straight up. WATERMARKS LEFT SIDE, F8. At (A) climb up and slightly left into a small inside corner below an overhang, step out right, and the rest is easy.
5 DER GLOTZ, F9A. Start on the face 10 feet left of Watermarks, below a faint slanting dihedral a few inches wide. Follow this line past the left end of the overhang noted in Watermarks Left Side.
6 SUNKEN PILLAR, F6. Start at the double cracks, stem up until the cracks diverge; from here you can follow either one. The climb ends near the base of Balanced Rock.

Diagram XIII E

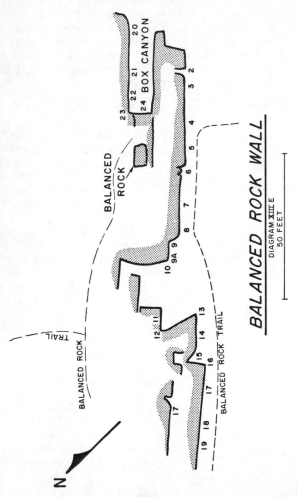

BALANCED ROCK WALL

Diagram XIII E
50 FEET

100

7   RED PULPIT, F6. Start at a thin crack 5 feet left of the two oaks. Climb crack (harder for short people) and step right onto the pulpit 20 feet up, continue left and up past a juniper to top. AAHRG, F9A. Start at the large oak, climb face straight up to the pulpit.

8   FEAR AND TREMBLING, F9A. Start on face just right of corner. The first section of 10 feet is quite difficult; after this, continue up crack and wall (close to corner) to large ledge 15 feet below top, climb remaining smooth wall to top. Variation, F7. Start as in the Red Pulpit, traverse left onto Fear And Trembling, thus avoiding the direct start.

9   F5. Climb the inside corner until it becomes a crack, continue the crack or step off onto easier rock on the right.

9A   F6. Climb the wall and corner left of the inside corner.

10   MUCKY GULLY, F3. A dirty access gully that is a simple scramble (in dry weather). A little harder if you stay in the right corner (instead of turning left halfway up).

11   F9A. Start from the dirt and rock slope on the left side of Mucky Gully. Climb the wall (a couple of feet right of the inside corner) into a shallow dihedral (crux) and to top.

12   F5. Inside corner with projecting chockstone.

13   GRANDMA'S STAIRCASE, F6. Climb the corner on easy ledges to the overhang (leave grandma here), step right, climb face (left of inside corner, route 12) to top.

14   SPRING FEVER, F8. This is not a clearly defined line. Start up center of steep lower slab to the overhang. Do not go into the niche (route 15), instead step up right past the overhang, continue by lay-backing the steep narrow section above (note the loose flake hold).

15 BIFURCATION, F4. Climb the slab through notch on left side (chockstone in notch) and into alcove above. Step left onto a bouldery bench and continue to top. Variation, F6. Climb right crack inside the alcove.

16 F9A. Overhanging corner.

17 INVITATION, F6. Start below the obvious crack, climb crack to bench above. For a continuation, climb onto a sharp block and retable to top. INVITATION INDIRECT, F8. Start same as Invitation, follow thin crack left into notch at top of the wall.

18 F9A. Climb straight up wall into the notch noted above.

19 F8. Climb short wall 5 feet from west end.

BOX CANYON (Diagram XIII E)

20 F5. A relatively long route that starts at low point of the wall below Box Canyon. Climb the corner and somewhat slabby wall 35 feet to a ledge, up an easy inside corner to another ledge, then any of several continuations as desired. Variation, F6. At the 35-foot ledge, step left and climb the obvious jam crack.

21 F5. Climb one of the cracks in the north wall of Box Canyon.

22 THE BALANCE CLIMB, F7. Climb the smooth wall (about 5 feet right of the inside corner) to the level of Balanced Rock platform. Continue the same line over a bulge to platform above.

23 THE GARGOYLE, F5. Climb the inside corner, either traversing to Balanced Rock or continuing the inside corner past the projecting chockstone. Variation. Starting from Balanced Rock, you can do a "blind" traverse into the inside corner then up past the chockstone as before.

24 F6. Short jam crack that leads to Balanced Rock.

25 THE SQUIGGLE, etc. (no diagram). Start on the
platform 15 feet above Balanced Rock. Traverse 40
feet east along a ledge above Box Canyon, and turn
north around corner to a pine tree. There are several possibilities here, including: F6. Climb a crack
behind the pine tree . . . . F5. "Squiggle" up behind
(or climb outside of) a chockstone 10 feet east of the
pine tree.

BALANCED ROCK RIDGE (no diagram)

This is a series of walking and scrambling pitches,
leading from Balanced Rock to the bluff top 200 feet
above. Except for a couple of short variations the
climbing is pretty trivial. Balanced Rock itself can be
ascended on the east side or northeast corner. It is a
one-move climb, especially if you are tall enough to
reach the top immediately.

There are other rocks east of the immediate Balanced Rock area, but only a few routes are worth
describing. East Bluff elevation, west section, might be
helpful in locating the following rocks (no diagram):

LIEDERKRANZ, F6, A1. Walk around the east end
of Balanced Rock Wall and up the gully 100 feet. On
the right there is a 45-foot outcropping with an
overhanging block. Ascend ledges until beneath east
side of the block, traverse left (stepping in a sling), and
climb west corner of the block to top.

F6. Layback crack below west side of the block.

HOLE-IN-THE-WALL, F6. This is 100 yards east of
Balanced Rock, on a smooth wall facing southeast.
Climb crack through a shallow square niche.

F7. On same wall, 25 feet right of the niche, a layback
crack leading to a shallow dihedral. There are several
other climbs on this wall, and also some around the
lower (south) corner.

THE SLAB. Hike up lower bluff midway between Balanced Rock and Devil's Doorway. Above the main boulderfield find a 35-foot slab (two routes).

THE EFFIE, F7. Above The Slab is a wall facing southwest. The Effie (a memorial to Effinger Beer, once brewed in Baraboo) is an inside corner/jam crack that starts with an overhang. Negotiate the overhang without using the large detached block on the left.

F7. Climb the face directly above this block.

Railroad Tracks Area

Above the east shore of the lake, roughly midway between the south and north shores, are a number of outcroppings affording excellent climbing. Many of the climbs are down low, a feature that is appreciated on hot summer days. Carry a swim suit in your pack. The major outcroppings are the RAILROAD AMPHITHEATER, the BIRTHDAY ROCKS, and HORSE RAMPART. These are all near the "electric fence," a net that parallels the railroad tracks for several hundred feet to give warning in the event of rockfall onto the track.

The RAILROAD AMPHITHEATER is near the bottom of the bluff 150 feet north of the electric fence. It is notable for its overhanging north wall and for two fairly long climbs on its south wall. Slopes to the south and north of the whole outcropping give access to the top of the amphitheater. THE LUMBY RIDGE is a traditional route consisting of short pitches that ascend the rocks at the south end of the amphitheater, ending on THE TURRET above. Also on this upper level is WATERFALL WALL, a formation with rounded ledges and contours. The BLASTED ROCK is a steep 50-foot wall 200 feet north of the Railroad Amphitheater; the climbing is on sloping crackless rock atypical of Devil's Lake. Recommended climbs in the Railroad Amphitheater: Snedegar's Nose, F7; Cop-Out, F10A; Catenary Crack, F9A; Pine Tree Step-Across, F6.

The BIRTHDAY ROCKS are in the area above the electric fence. The main southwest wall starts 50 feet above the fence and angles up (southeast) to a prominent tower. A parallel rock band on the slope immediately above this is much more broken, but can be explored for a few routes. Recommended climbs: Horner's Corner, F5; Birthday Crack, F7; Caesarian Tower, F8.

HORSE RAMPART is above the large boulderfield just south of the electric fence. It is a higher southward continuation of the band that forms the upper part of the Railroad Amphitheater and Birthday Rocks. The culminating point at the south end of the rampart is TEETERING TOWER. Other rocks in the area include LOTHAR'S LEDGES, a series of rock steps on the boulderfield above and south of the electric fence, and SQUIRREL'S NEST TOWER, a 50-foot formation 100 yards south of Horse Rampart. This tower is seldom climbed but is very worthwhile. It can also be reached from the opposite direction by contouring 200 yards north from Balanced Rock Wall. Recommended climbs: Roger's Roof, F8; Treachery, F7; Debauchery, F8; Primak's Surprise, F?.

Other rocks of the east shore: The outcroppings already described fall on the two lowest rock bands above the east shore. There is a third band that starts above the Horse Rampart and extends south almost to the summit near Balanced Rock Trail. A fourth band consists of summit rocks that appear intermittently on the north half of the bluff (Elephant Rock, Tomahawk Rock). Both upper bands are fairly broken and rarely climbed. They would provide ground for someone interested in exploring.

RAILROAD AMPHITHEATER (Diagram XIV E)

1 SNEDEGAR'S NOSE, F7. Ridge route. Start right side of corner, step left and up onto block at base of the ridge, stem 10 feet on right side, continue steep slab climbing on or just left of ridge corner.

2 JACK THE RIPPER, F9B. For those who enjoy self-abuse. Start below a diagonal gash, jam up the gash, and reach ridge about halfway up the wall.

3 COP-OUT, F10A. A study in combinatorial climbing. Start 10 feet left of The Pillar, climb thin cracks 35 feet into inside corner beneath overhang, step onto right corner, and climb to top.

4 CATENARY CRACK, F9A. A swooping curve that yields to deep analysis. Start 5 feet left of The Pillar, climb crack to top of wall.

5 THE PILLAR, F6. Climb or chimney up the standing block. Step across into upper half of Catenary Crack. Variation, F8. From The Pillar climb upper wall to right of Catenary Crack. Note: a 20-foot wall (routes 7 and 8) can be climbed to reach next level.

6 Deleted.

9 PINE TREE STEP-ACROSS, F6. Start 5 feet left of inside corner (route 10), climb onto first sloping ledge, shuffle left to corner, continue up and right onto overhanging block with pine tree, step *far* left and feel for handhold to pull yourself across, continue up slabby rock to top. Variation. Start in the inside corner, but traverse left on black rock and then climb up to the pine tree.

10 PINE TREE DIHEDRAL, F5. Climb inside corner below pine tree block, move right out of the overhang and up to next ledge, continue the inside corner past two more ledges to top.

11 F5.

12 F7. Inside corners obscured by trees.

13 FACE-OFF, F9A. Start on upper right end of

Diagram XIV E

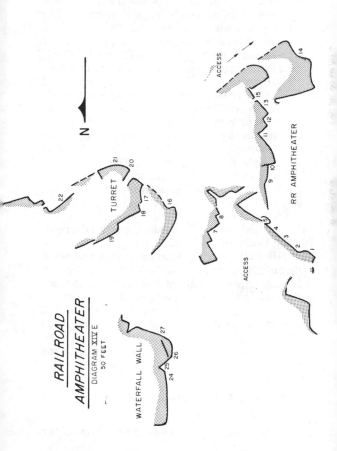

detached block, step left onto the face, move up and left toward corner, where climbing becomes easier.

14 LUMBY RIDGE, named after Harry Lumby, a former CMC president who suffered a heart attack on these rocks on a hot Saturday morning while exerting himself on a layback. The ridge is a traditional route consisting of short pitches. The start is only a few feet from the RR tracks. Climb onto loose upright plate and up crack to first platform. Continue as follows: **15**. Climb chimney from bottom or traverse into it from adjacent inside corner, to reach next platform. Do a step-across (over a gap) to the north going around into a short chimney and up. Walk to next low wall **(16)** and up onto a sloping platform. **17**. Step onto left end of large displaced block, go right and up onto a little slab and climb to summit platform. A hole in the platform gives access to scramble route down south side.

18 F5. Short corner.

19 F6. Climb short face or inside corner on the right.

20 F4. Corner next to wide chimney.

21 THE TURRET, F7. Start on south corner below first overhang, or start on right side and climb or traverse onto corner above first overhang, to reach ledge 15 feet up that extends to the left. Continue somewhat right on south side to top of The Turret, or step left on the ledge and finish on southwest side.

22 F4-F7. Short wall with two crack routes and one inside corner.

WATERFALL WALL (Diagram XIV E)

23 Deleted.

24 F7. Start up diagonal ledge (the right one of two

108

such ledges), climb crack to ledge beneath notched overhang, retable through the notch and up short steep wall to top.

25 F6. Inside corner and chimney.

26 DISAPPEARING LEDGE, F7. Climb corner to large ledge, move right and step up on wall above, traverse left on a disappearing ledge, continue up and left around the corner.

27 F8. Start on block and climb left up to a large ledge, continue right and up, staying close to southwest corner.

BIRTHDAY ROCKS (Diagram XV E)

1 HORNER'S CORNER, F5. Climb crack 20 feet to a bench, then up west wall and southwest corner, climbing from ledge to ledge. Beware: sitting on a ledge is indecorous and subject to penalty.

2 F7. Thin crack in recessed section.

3 F7. Face climb.

4 F5. Ledges and crack that end left of 15-foot upper corner.

5, 6 F7. Both climbs are in shallow inside corners leading to an overhang.

7 F10A. Wall left of Birthday Crack.

8 BIRTHDAY CRACK, F7. A prominent crack with overhang at the ledge one-third of the way up.

9 F4. Chimney.

10 CAESARIAN TOWER, F8. Start on first ledge, climb the sharp west corner or adjacent groove to higher ledge on northwest side, climb right onto the overhanging upper corner (the key is keeping hand in left crack), shinny to top of tower.

11 SPECIAL DELIVERY, F6. Climb chockstone crack in the hanging inside corner.

12 BIRTHDAY BOULDER, F9A. Face route.

Caesarian Tower (route 10, diagram XV E)

Diagram XV E

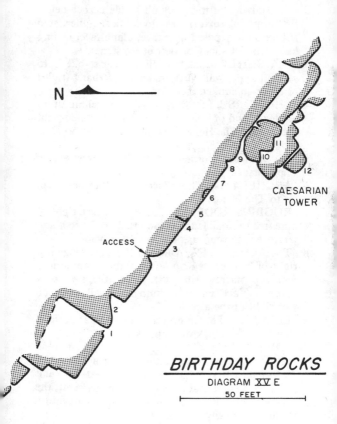

N

ACCESS

CAESARIAN
TOWER

BIRTHDAY ROCKS

DIAGRAM XV E

50 FEET

HORSE RAMPART (Diagram XVI E)

1 F8. Corner above low slab.

2 F7. Narrow buttress. Climb inside corner below first overhang, exit right onto south shoulder, step left onto the exposed west face, climb face, ending on northwest shoulder (left of capstone).

3 F9A. Start left of oak tree, climb steep slab (F7), to vertical upper wall, then up small overhang (right) or crack in sunken face (left).

4 THE HORSE, F5. Start by oak tree, climb up to left (east) end of large flake (The Horse), step right and mount The Horse (or vice versa), up corner to top.

5 F7. Start near corner and climb past west end of The Horse.

6 ARCHERY, F8. Climb face (just left of pine tree) up to The Horse.

7 ROGER'S ROOF, F8. Climb rib 4 feet right of pine tree to small ledge below crack in the roof and jam over the roof, using a knee if it helps.

8 TREACHERY, F7. Waltz up 10 feet to ledge just right of alcove, step up left, painfully jamming a foot, up narrow rib past birch tree into easy chimney. Variation, F7. Climb lower wall, staying 6 feet right of the alcove.

9 LECHERY, F8. Climb crack to ledge at 25 feet, finish in thin crack on upper wall.

10 DEBAUCHERY, F8. Pure undistorted climbing (deficient in protection). Climb on or near corner for 25 feet past first ledge, move a few feet left, and pull onto a comfortable ledge. Above this point, the corner is ill-defined; continue slightly right into a shallow concavity for the final 20 feet.

11 PRIMAK'S SURPRISE. To rate this climb would spoil the surprise. Every 10 feet you think you have passed the crux. Climb the inside corner, switch-backing holds on either side when it proves helpful.

Roger's Roof (route 7, diagram XVI E)

113

Diagram XVI E

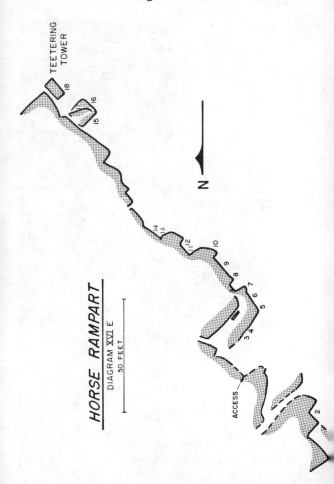

HORSE RAMPART

DIAGRAM XVI E

50 FEET

TEETERING TOWER

ACCESS

N

12 PLETHORA, F10A. Stem up inside corner past slight bulge on left wall to ledge 20 feet from top, climb the ugly overhanging crack to a cedar tree.

13 F5. Up inside corner onto left block, then up well-fractured rock to top.

14 VIA APIA, F7. Jam crack.

15 MUNG, F9A. Crack system in the northwest face.

16 F8. Left corner above ledge.

17 MOTHER SMUCKER'S JAM, F8. Overhanging jam crack.

18 TEETERING TOWER, F9A. A 40-foot tower separated from the main wall by a jumpable gap. There is a bolt at the top for anchoring a belay. The climb on the northwest corner is F7, except for the start, which is F9. (There was an easier start at the south corner until a hold broke off.)

LOTHAR'S LEDGES (no diagram)

Named for Lothar Kolbig, a former CMC president who was active in the 1940s and 1950s. This is a series of three rock steps in sequence, on the boulderfield above the electric fence (below Horse Rampart). There are a number of short climbs, including a fall-across from the first tower to the next wall. It is good place to take beginners, since each step has at least one easy climb.

SQUIRREL'S NEST TOWER (no diagram)

A 50-foot outcropping at mid-level on the bluff, 100 yards south of the Teetering Tower. It can also be approached from the opposite direction by contouring 200 yards north from Balanced Rock Wall. The southwest side has the following closely spaced routes (right to left):

115

F7. Inside corner and hanging chimney near south corner.

F7. Wide crack with remains of tree stump.

F7, F8. Left half of southwest face, two routes up the overhang.

F9A. Start from ledge on northwest side, step right to west corner, then up the corner.

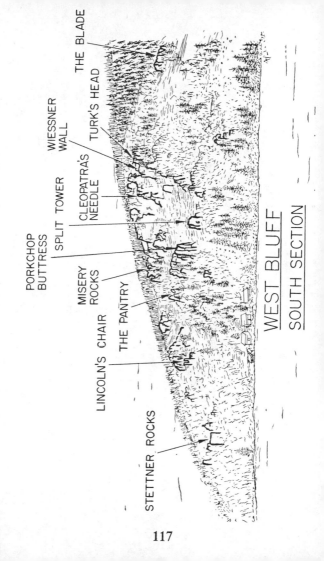

THE BLADE

WIESSNER WALL

TURK'S HEAD

SPLIT TOWER

CLEOPATRA'S NEEDLE

PORKCHOP BUTTRESS

MISERY ROCKS

LINCOLN'S CHAIR

THE PANTRY

STETTNER ROCKS

WEST BLUFF

SOUTH SECTION

117

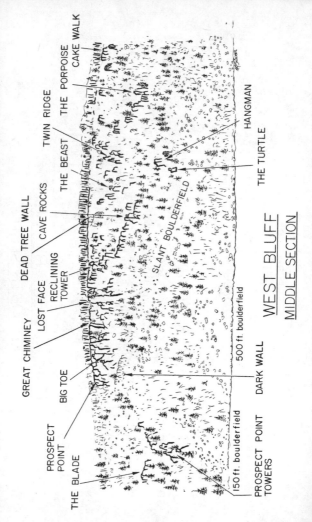

WEST BLUFF
MIDDLE SECTION

CAKE WALK
THE PORPOISE
TWIN RIDGE
THE BEAST
CAVE ROCKS
DEAD TREE WALL
RECLINING TOWER
LOST FACE
GREAT CHIMNEY
BIG TOE
PROSPECT POINT
THE BLADE
HANGMAN
THE TURTLE
SLANT BOULDERFIELD
500 ft. boulderfield
DARK WALL
150 ft. boulderfield
PROSPECT POINT TOWERS

118

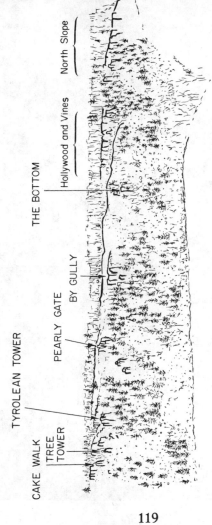

CAKE WALK

TREE TOWER

TYROLEAN TOWER

PEARLY GATE

THE BOTTOM

BY GULLY

Hollywood and Vines

North Slope

WEST BLUFF
NORTH SECTION

119

West Bluff

THE WEST BLUFF

Climbing on the West Bluff has the same general character as climbing elsewhere at Devil's Lake. There is perhaps a greater proportion of short climbs and climbs of moderate difficulty on the West Bluff. The outcroppings are widely scattered and often obscured by trees, making it difficult to locate and identify particular outcroppings; for this reason a quite detailed description of the major rock groups and the approaches to them is presented below.

The early climbing on the West Bluff (1940s) was generally limited to a few favorite spots. Recently the area has received renewed attention, and the less well-known sections were systematically examined by members of the Chicago Mountaineering Club. By now all the rock groups have been explored, though undoubtedly individual routes remain to be worked out. Note that many climbs listed have been done only once or twice, so the ratings of difficulty must be regarded as tentative and subject to adjustment.

The West Bluff outcroppings show a banded structure which dips to the north in the same manner as the outcroppings on the opposite shore. For the most part the bands are not continuous; they consist of rock patches interrupted by wooded slopes. In a few places the outcroppings form vertical extensions, providing relatively continuous ascent routes for 200 to 300 feet; for example, Turk's Head Ridge and Prospect Point Towers.

Major Rock Groups of the West Bluff

THE STETTNER ROCKS are at the far south end of the West Bluff, a region of southeast exposure and low elevation that has the advantage of a short approach. The rocks form a reddish band 200 feet long. The climbs are mostly short (20-30 feet) but of considerable variety, and are therefore often used for instruction.

LINCOLN'S CHAIR is a minor rock cluster 300 feet north of Stettner's Rocks, still on a relatively low section of the bluff. There are climbs of 20-35 feet on several levels, another suitable "school rocks" area for climbing parties.

The MISERY ROCKS are above the cottages at the southwest corner of Devil's Lake. The traditional FAT MAN'S MISERY climb is on the 40-foot summit wall of this region. The wall is distinguished by a large reclining block (THE PILLOW) that creates a cave-like enclosure. Directly below the summit wall is THE PANTRY, an outcropping with an alcove and ancillary walls and towers on two levels. Recommended climbs on these rocks: Weeping Wall, F9A; False Perspective, F6; Fat Man's Misery, F5; The Pillow, F6; Pantry Shelf, F7.

DUTCHMAN RAMPART is a south-facing wall across a gully 100 feet north of the Misery Rocks. It features a prominent high roof and a three-section tower (THE FRIGATE) at the east end. At a lower level are DUNGEON WALL, PORKCHOP BUTTRESS, and SPLIT TOWER. Porkchop Buttress is an impressive formation with relatively long climbs, 60-70 feet. Split Tower is an isolated 40-foot outcropping 150 feet north of Porkchop, on a line below Cleopatra's Needle. Recommended climbs include: Oh Rats, F8; Can-Can, F6; Flying Dutchman, F9A; The Bone, F5; Moon Face, F7.

The CLEO AMPHITHEATER is part of the upper-most band on the south portion of the West Bluff. The Amphitheater is 200 feet across and partly surrounds a 50-foot spire, CLEOPATRA'S NEEDLE. These rocks are densely covered with routes, some of the best being: Barndoor, F8; King's Throne, F6; Queen's Throne, F5; Queen's Face, F8; Cleopatra's Needle (southeast side), F5.

WIESSNER WALL and TURK'S HEAD form a northerly extension of the Cleo Amphitheater; they are perhaps the most prominent of the southern rocks. Wiessner Wall is over 60 feet high, but it is naturally broken into two pitches. Turk's Head can be seen in jutting profile from points along the south shore. There are additional climbs of the same rock band up to 100 feet north of Turk's Head, and a separate outcropping, THE BLADE, 300 feet to the north. Outstanding climbs include: Wiessner Face, F7; Green Slime, F9A; Turk's Tooth (north ledges), F4; The Blade, F6.

TURK'S HEAD RIDGE ascends most of the bluff below Turk's Head, ending at TURK'S TOOTH. It provides a nearly continuous sequence of moderate pitches.

PROSPECT POINT TOWERS form a ridge that extends up the middle third of the bluff below Prospect Point. It is a magnificent formation with fine climbs: Track Cracks, F8; Sun-Top, F8; The Great Crack, F6; Garden Path, F7.

PROSPECT POINT RAMPART is the summit cliff on the central part of the West Bluff. The cliff is continuous from Prospect Point to Lost Face 400 feet to the north. The average height of the cliff is about 80 feet, but it is broken by many benches and ledges. In a few places it does provide long continuous climbs, notably at the GREAT CHIMNEY and LOST FACE. At the base of the rampart is the somewhat distinct DARK WALL, encountered when ascending a little north from Prospect Point Towers. Climbs include: Grand Illusion, F8; Stuck Knee, F7; Son of Great

Chimney, F10A; Lost Face, F6; Lost Face Overhang, F8.

RECLINING TOWER and DEAD TREE WALL are short separate sections of the summit cliff north of the main Prospect Point Rampart. The latter is the more impressive formation, a steep wall with climbs of up to 60 feet. From Reclining Tower, a minor band (CAVE ROCKS RAMPART) extends northeast halfway down the bluff, ending at the CAVE ROCKS. These rocks and those further north (described below) are climbed quite infrequently. Recommended climbs: Reclining Tower Arete, F6; Dead Tree Climb, F8.

HANGMAN TOWERS. This group north of the Dead Tree Wall includes the TWIN RIDGE, THE PORPOISE, and other rocks scattered over several hundred feet on the upper half of the bluff. The climbs are all in the short category, up to 30 feet. The outcroppings end to the north where a talus slope covers much of the upper bluff.

TREE TOWER and TYROLEAN TOWER are 200 feet apart, both a little below the crest of the bluff. There are summit walls of interest behind the Tree Tower. The Tyrolean Tower (top first reached by Tyrolean traverse) has long been ascended only with "artificial" aid; a free-climbing route was found only recently. Recommended climbs: Bowler's Grip, F8; Koala Bear, F10A; Der Schnozzel, F8.

North end of the West Bluff. Beyond the Tyrolean Tower there are only a couple of isolated climbs until one reaches the region above the north end of the lake. Here the rocks range mainly in three bands: BY GULLY, HOLLYWOOD AND VINES, and NORTH SLOPE. The most southerly of these bands, By Gully, has just a few routes. The other two bands are more extensive, each extending for several hundred feet immediately beneath the West Bluff Trail. The climbs on both bands are typically 30-40 feet long.

WEST BLUFF APPROACHES

The present WEST BLUFF TRAIL (summit trail) begins at the junction of the south shore road and the cottage access road, at the southwest corner of the lake. The first (south) part of the trail is asphalt. Formerly the trail began a few hundred feet to the east; this old "climbers' trail" is convenient for reaching some of the southern rocks of the West Bluff, since it follows the bluff crest more closely than the newer official trail. Useful landmarks along the West Bluff Trail (using the old variation to start) are described below. Distances noted below are between consecutive points.

A. Trail head (unmarked) is by the third utility pole along the cottage access road, 325 feet east from the south shore road.

B. (300 feet) The trail reaches a bench above the first minor rock band. The Stettner Rocks are 100 feet northeast at this level.

C. (925 feet) The trail passes a vantage point that can be identified by a "slingshot" pine tree growing on the summit wall of the Misery Rocks, 50 feet east of trail. The trail passes a similar vantage point 300 feet before the Misery Rocks, in the vicinity of Lincoln's Chair.

D. (300 feet) The old trail merges with the new one at a point above Cleopatra's Needle; a couple of short gullies leading down to the Needle are found by walking north along the rim. Wiessner Wall and Turk's Head are accessible about 200 feet farther north. There is an unmarked path beaten by hikers leaving the established trail above Turk's Head; this path gradually descends to the north for 400 feet until it passes above The Blade, then turns down the gully adjacent to the Prospect Point Towers.

E. (1000 feet) Prospect Point. This vantage point has a panorama that includes the whole of Devil's Lake. Prospect Point Rampart is the summit wall below and to the north of this point. To the south there is a broad summit boulderfield which occupies a hollow or break in the contour of the upper bluff.

F. (300 feet) Geodetic survey marker. (A park service road goes west from here to join the south shore road.) The Great Chimney is 50 feet south of the marker, the access gully to Lost Face is 75 feet north.

G. (325 feet) Trail splits into two branches; along the less used west branch are the remains of a small stone shelter. Reclining Tower is 150 feet south of the branching point, Dead Tree Wall 100 feet north. There is an access gully to the south of each formation.

H. (525 feet) The two branches (which split at G) reunite. Go-Go Tower is 100 feet below this point, Twin Ridge 150 feet farther south. These rocks (and others of the Hangman Towers) are not generally visible from the bluff top. About 200 feet to the north a boulderfield appears on the upper bluff, reaching almost to the summit.

I. (425 feet) Trail passes the Tree Tower. Though only 50 feet off the summit, the tower is easy to miss because of intervening trees; it has a small pine tree near its top. There is a rather steep rock access route in the summit wall behind the Tree Tower.

J. (175 feet) An elevated vantage point, overlooking the Tyrolean Tower, which is barely discernible about 75 feet below. There is a short rise in the trail approaching this point from the south.

K. (325 feet) Another vantage point. The rocks immediately below have no interesting climbs. However, 150 feet to the north is the Pearly Gate. This is not visible from the trail; look for a little descending cleft that leads 25 feet to the edge of the bluff above this wall.

L. (350 feet) Dip in the trail where it crosses the head of a large gully. There is a wall, By Gully, about 100 feet down on the north side. Just north of the gully a path branches off from the summit trail; it soon fades out.

M. (325 feet) Trail division point. The easterly branch is another false trail that follows a bench below the summit, eventually to become lost on a talus slope. It is often used since one can continue down boulders directly to the north shore beach area. For a stretch this branch trail parallels the base of Hollywood and Vines, a summit band that arises 200 feet north of the division point.

N. (650 feet) North Slope. A descending section of the trail about 225 feet long, with rock slabs along the edge of the bluff. The cliff below is the final rock band along the summit trail; 375 feet farther north the trail ends at the north shore road.

TUMBLED ROCKS TRAIL (the shore trail) starts at the south end of the West Bluff where the cottage access road ends. The most convenient and pleasant approaches using this trail are as follows:

A. Cottage road. 200 feet before reaching the north end of the road, turn up (northwest) on the least overgrown talus in the area; this leads into a gully in the Misery Rocks.

B. Trail head (at end of cottage road). Double Chimney and Porkchop Buttress are 200-300 feet above this point; to reach them it is easier to go 100 feet north along the trail to a point where a faint path goes up.

C. (350 feet) Turk's Head Ridge. Trail passes beneath the base of the ridge, a small tower 200 feet up the bluff.

D. (200 feet) Pat's Ridge. The first tower is the

lowest rock outcropping in the area; from the trail it appears as a two-tier sloping block.

E. 150-foot (wide) boulderfield, the first large open patch of boulders that the trail crosses. Ascend the boulders, turning a little south to reach the base of Prospect Point Tower, or hike up about 250 feet on a faint path in the woods south of this boulderfield.

F. 500-foot (wide) boulderfield, a large patch 100 feet north of the 150-foot boulderfield. High above are the summit cliffs north of Prospect Point. Various sections of the cliffs can be reached as follows:

(1) Ascend south edge of the 500-foot boulderfield, continue over and between large blocks onto the slant boulderfield on the upper bluff; follow the slant boulderfield southwest toward Prospect Point or go up through trees to the summit band in the vicinity of the Great Chimney.

(2) Ascend north portion onto the upper reach of the 500-foot boulderfield, then bear somewhat north to avoid most of the trees, passing a 25-foot rock with a steep slab climb. This brings you up to a low rock band, the Cave Rocks Rampart; follow the rampart southwest to Reclining Tower, or cross it northwest to the Dead Tree Wall.

G. The Turtle. North of the 500-foot boulderfield the trail passes through a gradually narrowing strip of trees. Near the north end of the strip, on the open slope above (slant boulderfield) one can see The Turtle, a large sloping rock with a small boulder at the top. The Cave Rocks are about 250 feet southwest of The Turtle. Hangman Towers cover an extensive area above The Turtle.

H. Slant boulderfield. This is the third large patch that the trail crosses. It extends diagonally south, following the tilt of the rock strata, practically uninterrupted to Prospect Point. Starting where the trail emerges from the trees, go upward across this field, then continue up on fairly open talus to a rock band 2/3 way up the bluff; this is The Porpoise. You can now veer north across a higher boulderfield to reach the summit in the vicinity of the Tree Tower.

WEST BLUFF ROCK CLIMBS

STETTNER ROCKS (Diagram I W)

ACCESS: Starting from the cottage road, hike up the old West Bluff Trail 300 feet to a bench above the first minor rock band. On this level follow a path 100 feet northeast to base of the Stettner Rocks.

1   F8. Short face climb.
2   F6. Overhang at southwest corner of west buttress. Climb up left of a small sharp rib underneath the overhang. Variation, F8. Climb on right side of the rib.
2A F4. Southwest corner. Follow good ledges to top.
3   F5. Climb 15 feet past minor crux into easy upper chimney.
4   F7. Southeast side of west buttress, a relatively unbroken face ascended on small ledges.
5-8 Short climbs.
9   THE NICHE, F5. Climb an inside corner to the niche, retable out to the left or hand-traverse farther left to an easier spot. There is a practice traverse between climbs 9 and 12 that is just off the ground and can be done unroped.
10 THE MANTELSHELF, F8. Start up roughly on the midline of the wall to reach the first ledge. The problem on this line is the smaller ledge 5 feet higher; an indirect approach is to traverse onto it from one end or the other (the direct approach is left as a student exercise).
11 Deleted.
12 F4. Chimney.
13 F6. Follow bucket holds 2 feet right of the chimney, a bit overhanging.
14 F9A. Overhang on south side of Beastly Bulge.

130

Diagram I W

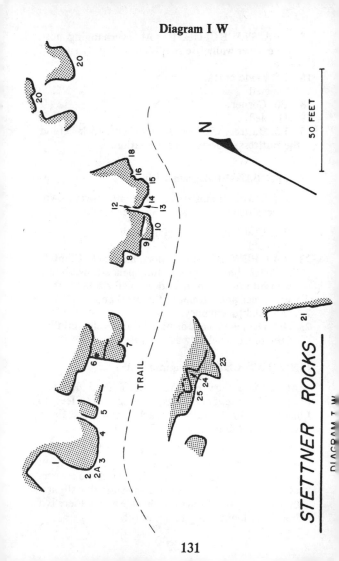

STETTNER ROCKS

50 FEET

131

15 BEASTLY BULGE, F7. An overhanging nose on the lower wall. Use small holds slightly right of center.

16 F5. Wide crack.

17 Deleted.

18 F6. Corner.

19 Deleted.

20 F3. Buttress with easy ledges. Some rock behind the buttress provides a continuation.

LOWER BAND (Diagram I W)

The following climbs are on some rather overgrown, dirty rocks below the regular Stettner Rocks.

21 F5. Crack in a wall facing southwest.

22 Deleted.

23 OLD PEW, F7. Start: A diagonal crack. Climb to first ledge, balance up carefully beneath overhang, reach into notch above and grope for a hold, then stand erect and surmount the overhang.

24 F5. Slabby chimney.

25 F7. Detached block on upper wall. Follow midline of the block as closely as possible.

LINCOLN'S CHAIR (Diagram II W)

ACCESS: Follow old West Bluff Trail 600 feet beyond the Stettner Rocks, descend 100 feet to Lincoln's Chair. Can also be reached from the Misery Rocks area, 200 feet south of The Pantry.

1 LINCOLN'S CHAIR (south arm), F5. (The two arms are 30 feet high and 10 feet apart.) Start on south corner, end somewhat left around the corner.

2 F6. Southeast face of south arm. Start this slightly overhanging face from the right side where there is a hold that looks ready to break off.

Diagram II W

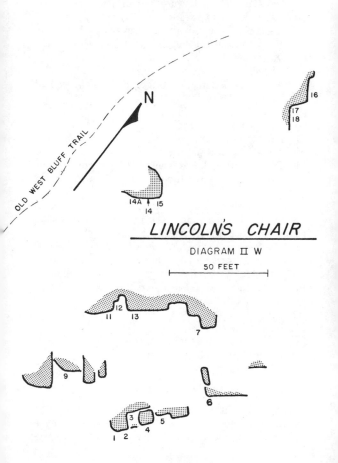

N

OLD WEST BLUFF TRAIL

14A 14 15

LINCOLN'S CHAIR

DIAGRAM II W

50 FEET

16
17
18

11 12 13

7

9

6

1 2 3 4 5

3 F4. Short inside corner crack above seat of the chair.

4 LINCOLN'S CHAIR (north arm), F5. Start on left corner of the arm or (a bit harder) on a little ramp on right corner, climb about halfway up, then move right to pass an overhang.

5-7 Short climbs.

8 Deleted.

9 F4. Recessed slab. Climb face of the slab or slant chimney on left side.

10 Deleted.

11 F5. Chockstone crack.

12 F5. Alcove. Climb south wall. The north chimney of the alcove is a scramble.

13 F4. 35-foot wall. Best route is 10 feet north of the alcove; farther north the wall is broken into short steps.

14 F5. Small compact outcropping near the local summit. It has a wide crack in the southeast side.

14A F6. Face 4 feet left of the wide crack.

15 F8. East corner. Climb on a line just left of the corner. Or start on right side of the corner, climb about 6 feet, then swing around to left side as before.

16 F7. Minor wall 60 feet north of preceding outcropping. Climb a 20-foot jam crack in a smooth face.

17 F5. Inside corner.

18 F7. Two cracks crossing a wide ledge. The lower left crack is F9A if it is climbed separately.

MISERY ROCKS (Diagram III W)

This wall forms the summit cliff in the region above the northernmost cottages. It is distinguished by a large reclining block, The Pillow, that forms a cave-like enclosure.

ACCESS is via the old West Bluff Trail. Up the trail 1/4 mile you pass the overlook above the Misery Rocks; the overlook can be identified by a "slingshot" pine tree. An alternative approach from below: 200 feet before reaching the end of the cottage road, start up the bluff on the fairly open talus that leads into the gully between the Misery Rocks and Dutchman Rampart.

1, 2 Deleted.

3 F7. Start with a layback move in a little inside corner, then easy rock above.

4 Deleted.

5 WEEPING WALL, F9A. Start at a slight ground-level niche, climb somewhat left on small holds with a delicate move 12 feet up, continue more easily, staying a few feet left of the adjacent crack (6).

6 FALSE PERSPECTIVE, F6. Shallow V-chimney and crack. Climb in the chimney or on left outside corner, then follow the crack continuation above. The crux is the transition from chimney to crack.

7 FAT MAN'S MISERY, F5. Start 10 feet inside the "cave" behind The Pillow, climb the rear (west) wall until you get into a chimneying position facing east, work out of the cave and up to the tight chimney at the south end of The Pillow. (The upper chimney becomes Any Man's Misery if you are trapped by leaning in too far.)

8 F7. South end of The Pillow. Start on a pointed rock, climb the narrow south end of both lower and upper blocks.

9 THE PILLOW (southeast corner and overhang), F6. Climb corner to overhang formed by upper block, attack the overhang by moving a bit right and taking a high step up. Variation, F6. At the overhang traverse left to the upper chimney of route 7.

135

Diagram III W

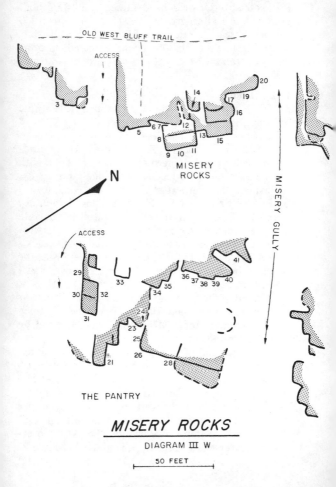

OLD WEST BLUFF TRAIL

ACCESS

3

ACCESS

N

MISERY GULLY

MISERY ROCKS

THE PANTRY

MISERY ROCKS

DIAGRAM III W

50 FEET

10 F4. Slab climb on outside of The Pillow. Follow good holds left of center, and escape right at overhang.

11 F6. North slab route. Climb at or near north edge of The Pillow.

12 SMOKE HOLE, F4. Climb the deep chimney behind The Pillow, exiting through hole at the top of the "cave."

13 F3. Chimney.

14 F4. Narrow prominence above north end of The Pillow; climb on south side or southeast ledges.

15 F5. Three 10-foot steps, taken at a crack that widens with each step.

16 F7. Climb 10 feet to a ledge bearing a large tree, continue up right-hand corner, go head first into the tight awkward chimney or climb on outside just right of the chimney.

17 F6. Long crack in left side of a dirty chute.

18 Deleted.

19 F7. Overhanging wall, not as impossible as it looks. Start near north end, work left on ledges, then upward with a difficult move to reach the highest ledge.

20 F8. Climb north end of the overhanging wall, which has a desperate move near the top. Licheny rock, often wet.

THE PANTRY (Diagram III W)

21 F6. Corner/crack. Climb just left of the corner to gain corner ledge, then angle right up the wide diagonal crack.

22 Deleted.

23 PANTRY SHELF, F7. Step up to the sloping shelf on the lower part of the wall (crux), continue in the left inside corner to the top overhang, finish straight up or go right beneath the overhang.

24 F4. Chimney with easy stemming.

25 F5. North wall of The Pantry.

26 PANTRY CORNER, F5. A pleasant climb on well-spaced holds.

27 Deleted.

28 F5. Cracks leading to a dead tree stump. Optional continuation: flaky crack 5 feet to the left in highest part of the wall.

29 F4. Crack and inside corner, an easy scramble.

30 SPECIAL K, F6. Climb a shallow chimney, overhang, and crack, ending at a ledge near the top of a small tower.

31 F5. Climb southeast flank of the tower in three short pitches. Descend on northwest side into the gap behind the tower.

32-35 Short climbs.

36 F7. Slight inside corner with small overhang.

37 F4. Cracks.

38 F6. Crack, narrowest at bottom.

39 F6. Overhang. Climb around north end of the overhang into an inside corner.

40 F7. Start: face or angling crack just left of the northeast corner. Climb 15 feet to a ledge, then up the northeast corner on sloping holds. There is an easier start behind the wall (at the northwest corner).

41 F5. Climb right wall of wide chimney.

DUTCHMAN RAMPART (Diagram IV W)

ACCESS is same as for Misery Rocks; Dutchman Rampart is at the north border of the Misery Rocks.

1 F6. Overhanging crack.

2 F5. Deep covered chimney. Getting out at the top is a messy procedure.

3   F6. Ledges/crack. Start on south side (left of the corner), climb to second large ledge, finish by a finger crack in a groove to left of Oh Rats roof.

4   OH RATS, F8. Traverse north from the large ledge noted above and climb a layback underneath the large upper overhang, escape by a hand pendulum onto the right-hand corner, end with delicate climbing just around the corner.

5   F4. Chimney with jutting overhangs, imposing in appearance but an easy climb. Stem up 30 feet, bear right through a cleft to west end of a bench. Variation, F5. Instead of bearing right, it is possible to work left to the large ledge of route 3, then continue by route 3 or 4.

6   F6. Narrow chimney, continuation of route 5.

7-11   Short climbs up to and above the bench that crosses Dutchman Rampart.

12   F6. Prominent upper section with overhang. Climb groove that leads behind a projecting block, surmount the overhang on substantial holds.

13   F7. Climb the prominent section near its right-hand corner; the hardest move is just below the top.

14   Deleted.

THE FRIGATE (Diagram IV W)

15   THE POOPER, F8. This is the overhanging west wall of The Frigate. Climb to a small triangular niche, hand pendulum right, then up the strenuous hanging crack that widens into a chimney.

16   CAN-CAN, F6. Climb 20 feet into a niche, climb out using a high left foothold, end in chimney that splits the high west end of The Frigate. Descent route, F4. From the west high point scramble east down to the midsection of The Frigate, then drop down a short crack (17) into the north saddle or continue down on the south side (20).

139

Diagram IV W

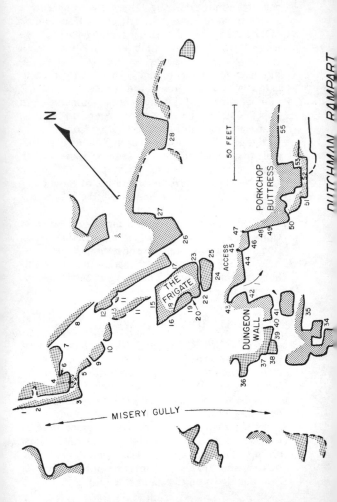

18 F8. Thin crack above west end of a platform.

19, 20 Easy cracks up to the platform and above.

21 Deleted.

22, 23 F4. Two chimney routes on opposite sides of The Frigate.

24 FLYING DUTCHMAN, F9A. Climb up under the right part of the southeast overhang, move left and up into a tight notch to stand on a little flake on the left outer wall, then up a nice face to the summit block, surmount block by a dynamic move at the obtuse southeast corner.

25 F8. Northeast corner of The Frigate. Start at the east corner, climb 15 feet, angling to the northeast corner (adjacent to the north chimney, 23), climb here to the base of the summit block, traverse left across the northeast side, balance onto a toehold, and retable to the top.

26 F4. Buttress with mostly easy ledges on the south side.

27 F5. Inside corner with crack variation.

28 F5. 40-foot wall split by crack, two routes.

29-32 Deleted.

DUNGEON WALL (Diagram IV W)

33-35 Broken rocks at base of Dungeon Wall. The dungeon has an entrance via chimney 34 and an escape window opening to the south.

36 F6. Protruding section, stay on outside.

37 F4. Broken chimney.

38 F5. South corner of Dungeon Wall, a pleasant line.

39 DUNGEON WALL, F7. Start by a thin crack 5 feet from right-hand corner. The strict face route avoids the right corner (40) but a more natural line incorporates some holds on the corner.

141

40 F7. Corner. Start on sloping steps and follow the corner closely.

41 F6. Face opposite a small tower. Start on left side of the face, angle right to a small inside corner, climb to upper ledge, thence by crack or right corner to top.

42-48 Climbs in the recessed section between Dungeon Wall and Porkchop Buttress. Some of these shorter climbs are more interesting than you might expect, for example, route 45, an inside corner (F7).

PORKCHOP BUTTRESS (Diagram IV W)

ACCESS: Ascend the bluff in the vicinity of the north end of the cottage road; easiest place is from trail 100 feet north of end of the road. The first sizable outcropping encountered is Double Chimney; the next one, halfway up the bluff, is Porkchop Buttress.

49 F8. South wall. Most of this wall is guarded by an impassable overhang. Start high up the slope by the base of crack 48, climb to the right in treacherous balance to reach a high ledge, then to top.

50 F7. Southeast crack and face. Climb the crack leading to south end of a large ledge, from here climb the upper face, ending by a short wide diagonal crack near the left corner.

51 JACOB'S LADDER, F6. Long inside corner. The first half is easy slabby climbing, with a slightly harder line 5 feet left of the inside corner. The steep upper section has a small overhang. Variation, F4. Avoid upper section by walking 10 feet left to an easy cleft.

52 THE BONE, F5. Start on right side of a smooth tapered face 20 feet high. Climb the steeply angling inside corner to a moderate overhang, follow corner crack to ledge below bulging upper section, move 5 feet right, surmount bulge to reach top. Variation, F7. From ledge below bulging section climb left corner to top.

53 NO EXIT, F7. Start (optionally) on a 15-foot wall at base of the buttress. Then climb a short thin crack or an inside corner (around to the right) to a sloping platform, continue to top overhang (crux), which is passed on the left.

54 Deleted.

55 F7. Shallow chimney and crack. Climb to point below a dead stump, balance left onto a ledge from which a couple of variations lead to the top.

There is a small outcropping (not on diagram) below southeast side of Porkchop Buttress. It has a crack climb (F5) notable because of a wobbly block.

DOUBLE CHIMNEY (no diagram)

A 40-foot formation on the lower bluff, 100 feet below Porkchop Buttress. It has two towers with two chimney routes:

F4. Stem up chimney behind the east tower.

F4. Climb the narrower chimney of the west tower.

F8. East side of east tower. Climb a couple of ledges, stretch far right to northeast corner and up.

F7. South face of west tower. Start near west corner, move up right, and climb center crack to top. Variation, F8. Climb southeast corner 15 feet, traverse left to center crack and up.

SPLIT TOWER (Diagram VII W). See diagram on page 155.

ACCESS: Walk 150 feet north from base of Porkchop Buttress, or descend about 150 feet from Cleopatra's Needle.

1   F4. Long chimney by which Split Tower is split.
2   HALF MOON, F7. Rounded overhanging section. Start on sloping ledges, climb a jam crack in the overhang, finish on southeast corner above.
3   MOON FACE, F7. An attractive face and crack route, the first 15 feet the most difficult. Variation, F5. Avoid the difficult part by starting in a short chimney or on adjacent rib (4) at northeast corner of the tower, then step left to the crack.
3A   F8. Corner at right side of the long chimney.
5   F5. Inside corner.
6-8   Deleted.
9-11   Small rocks below Split Tower.

CLEO AMPHITHEATER (Diagram V W)

ACCESS: (New) West Bluff Trail, ⅓ mile from south end. The trail first emerges from the woods and overlooks the lake at a point above the Cleo Amphitheater. The most convenient point of descent into the Amphitheater is the short chimney behind Cleopatra's Needle.

1   F7. Wall below a small tower. Climb ledges for 20 feet, then an angling crack (crux) to a wide ledge at the base of the tower; continue by route 4.
2   F3. Chimney.
3   F4. Set of ledges at south end of the small tower.
4   F6. From the wide ledge at base of the tower step up onto left end of a sloping shelf, climb face above. Variation. Move right on the shelf and climb an overhanging jam crack.

Diagram V W

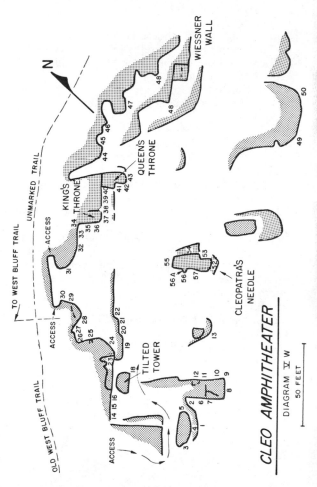

CLEO AMPHITHEATER

DIAGRAM V W

50 FEET

5 F8. North end of the tower is an overhanging corner, gained by a hand pendulum from a little chimney on the right.

6 F6. Crack.

7 F8. Short face climb leading to an inside corner.

8 F6. Buttress with two overhangs on southeast side. There is a choice of climbing left or right of the overhang in each case.

9 F8. Northeast corner, one of a group of severe routes (9-12) that cover the steep north face of the buttress.

10 F7. Crack 6 feet from northeast corner; toward top zag 3 feet to the right.

11 F8. Crack with layback move just left of a large niche.

12 F8. Stem up inside the niche, work out onto the face directly above, and climb to top.

13 F5. Short wall with 15-foot block at top. There are climbs on two sides.

14 F5. Start on dirty rock, end in one of two short chimneys 5 feet apart.

15 F6. The beginning of this climb is not well defined. Follow a line that higher up crosses two small overhangs.

16 PINKO, F7. Start in crack leading to a smooth face, balance up the face on small holds.

17 Deleted.

18 TILTED TOWER, F9A. Climb left edge of the severely overhanging north side of the tower.

19 F7. Climb 10 feet to a ledge, then up left crack containing a small tree. Variation, F8. Instead of the crack, ascend the rounded right-hand corner.

20 F5. Climb inside corner and crack, finishing on left side of a pointed overhang.

21 F5. Crack.

22 F5. Inside corner.

23 F8. Start from ledge on wall opposite top of Tilted Tower. At north end of the ledge step right to corner (instant exposure), climb corner to top.

24 BARNDOOR, F8. Follow crack to top of buttress, which is the highest point along the rim of the amphitheater.

25 F6. Narrow chimney.

26 COLOSTOMY, F6. A repulsive inside corner.

27 F4. Wide-angle inside corner. Climb left chimney or right crack.

28 THE PLANK, F8. Will you sink or swim when you walk The Plank? Start from the crack of route 27, traverse right just above the large ceiling, move around corner to reach ascent (or sudden descent) crack.

29 F8. Climb to a small niche at north end of the large ceiling, step into the niche, move left to corner and up. Variation, F8. From the niche, climb slightly right into an overgrown notch.

30 F7. Right side of northeast face. Climb to upper end of the diagonal crack.

31 F7. Curved wall. Climb 12 feet to a ledge, traverse left, and up (crux) near west end of the wall.

32 F5. Jam crack.

33 F5. Cracks 6 feet left of inside corner.

34 F4. Inside corner.

35 MISSING LINK, F8. This line is about 5 feet right of the inside corner (34), with the main problem between two ledges 12 feet apart.

36 F6. A set of out-sloping ledges.

37 KING'S THRONE, F6. The higher of two promontories that jut into the north half of Cleo Amphitheater. Climb the rounded corner on a series of evenly spaced horizontal cracks and ledges.

38 F6. Wide crack. At the top, continue 15 feet more on north side of the highest rock of the King's Throne.

39 F5. Crack with hardest move at bottom.

40 F5. Inside corner.

41 QUEEN'S THRONE, F5. A buttress crowned by a 6-foot rock spike. Climb the clean-cut inside corner/crack on comfortable ledges. An old favorite with nice exposure.

42 F9A. Climb on or just left of the corner; middle section is a bit overhanging.

43 QUEEN'S FACE, F8. East face of the Queen's Throne. The route keeps to the center of the narrow face.

44 F6. Crack/corner. Climb the angling crack part way, then up on right side of the corner.

45 F5. Chimney. Finish in left corner.

46 F5. Inside corner and face.

47 F7. 25-foot face. Climb left corner to top. Variation, F9C. Climb right corner of the face starting at a small niche.

48 F6. Corner, done in two pitches. Climb lower section by left crack or on right side of the corner.

49 F7. Buttress below north end of Cleo Amphitheater. Start at south corner or at overhang/crack to right of the south corner.

50 F7. Northeast side of the buttress, starting on the rounded corner.

51 Deleted.

CLEOPATRA'S NEEDLE (Diagram V W)

52 F5. Southeast side, the most popular route on Cleopatra's Needle. For esthetic reasons the climb is usually begun from a saddle on the northeast side rather than the lowest point. From the saddle cross over to the southeast side, climb (in one or two pitches) to base of the slender summit pinnacle, finish by nice face holds on southeast side or (a little easier) traverse around to north side just below top. (Note: other climbs listed below generally use one of these two finishes.)

53 F5. Inside corner.

54 F5. North ledges.

55 F5. Northwest side. Ascend right side of outsloping ledges, traverse left and up to base of summit block, finish on north side as in 52. This is the usual down-climbing route.

56 F7. Southwest rib. Climb bottom overhang to get onto outside of the rib, follow rib to ledge at base of summit block, move left and finish on northwest face of block.

56A F6. Inside corner/crack on left side of the southwest rib.

57 F5. Two cracks to right of the southeast rib. F6 if just the right crack is used.

TURK'S HEAD (Diagram VI W)

ACCESS: Starting where West Bluff Trail overlooks Cleopatra's Needle, follow an unmarked path 200 feet north, turn right down the bluff through a gully system on north side of Turk's Head. Or use the access routes into Cleo Amphitheater.

1 THE WASP, F7. Roof at south end of Wiessner Wall. Ascend ledges on the inner wall beneath the roof, traverse right (around corner) onto outer wall, ascend a jam crack to belay ledge with two small trees. Continue by one of the routes on the upper half of the wall (5-7).

2 F7. Start: a moderate crack 15 feet north of the roof. Climb crack 15 feet, move 5 feet left, and climb a thin face crack to belay ledge.

Diagram VI W

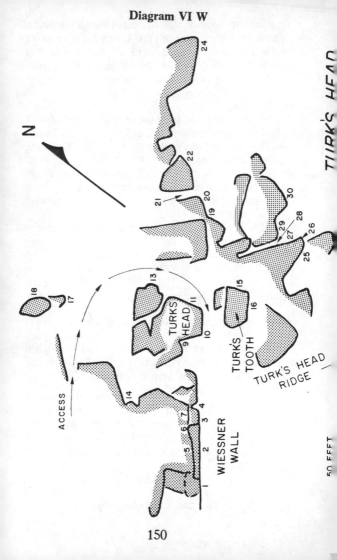

F5. Dirty chimney.
F6. Climb face and upper corner, staying a few feet right of the chimney.
F8. Face leading to V-chimney. It takes close examination to find the holds.

THE BLADE (Diagram VII W)

ACCESS: Start from top of bluff above Turk's Head, follow an unmarked path that gradually descends to the north; at about 300 feet it passes above The Blade.

1 Deleted.
2 F5. Overhang to left of central chimney.
3 F4. Chimney and adjacent rock, mostly easy.
4 F7. Crack climbed by layback and jamming.
5 F5. South corner of the main wall.
6 F6. Climb crack holding a small pine tree, continue straight up top overhang.
7 DEAR ABBEY, F8. Climb on small ledges to a niche at the center of the wall, step up into a thin crack, climb crack to top.
8 THE BLADE, F6. An acute-angled northeast corner. Step onto the corner from a block on the north side, continue on or near corner to top. Variation, F7. Finish via a thin crack 5 feet left of the corner.

TURK'S HEAD RIDGE (no diagram)

ACCESS: Tumbled Rocks Trail, 350 feet north of the cottages. Ascend bluff 200 feet to lowest outcropping visible above.

FIRST PITCH is a small tower with the following variations:

3 F8. Climb crack leading to niche, then climb on outside just left of the niche to reach exit crack above.
4 F5. Awkward narrow chimney that will seem harder if you don't find the right holds. Climb to base of small slab, traverse left to north end of belay ledge. Variation, F7. From base of the slab climb 10 feet on or near corner above, joining route 7.
5 F5. Starting from belay ledge, climb into shallow niche with sloping floor, continue up chockstone crack.
6 F4. Wide crack above north end of belay ledge. There may be loose rock in the crack, but the chief concern is likely to be wasp nests.
7 WIESSNER FACE, F7. A pretty variation on north part of the wall. From north end of belay ledge climb onto a bulge at base of the smooth upper face, then climb a set of horizontal cracks to top of the wall.
8 Deleted.
9 F4. Inside corner.
10 TURK'S HEAD (southeast corner), F5. Climb corner to overhang, finish on south side. Descend on south side or jump down from a short V-chimney on west side.
11 F6. Northeast ledges and overhang. Climb northeast side of Turk's Head to ledge beneath the wide overhang, reach up into central notch and mantel onto ledge above the overhang, walk around to south side for easiest way to top. Variation, F6. Surmount overhang by crawling onto shelf at north end. No one has ever looked good doing this.
12 Deleted.
13 F7. Rib with overhang; tackle the overhang from either side.
14 F4. Adjacent chimneys behind Turk's Head.

Wiessner Face (route 7, diagram VI W)

15 TURK'S TOOTH, F4. A tower just belo...
Head. The northeast side of this tower is a ...
ledge climb. Descend on the west side ...
Turk's Head).

16 F8. Overhang/chimney. Balance onto the ...
of a large flake from which the overhang ca...
be reached, move left and up into the ha...
chimney that breaches the overhang.

17 F5. Small tower. Climb east corner in two ...
tions, descend south crack.

18 F6. North face of the small tower.

19 F6. Crack/overhang. Climb 15 feet slightly l...
(following the crack), then up the overhang on tl...
right side of the crack. Variation, F7. Continue u...
the crack; surprisingly, this turns out to be harde...
than doing the overhang.

20 F7. Start at the same point as 19, work right ...
beneath the corner overhang, reach high and feel ...
for hold on the next ledge, surmount overhang, ...
proceed on the wall and ledges above.

21 F4. Chimney.

22 F6. Tower. Start on northeast side, or (better) ...
start near south corner and angle right across ...
southeast face. Mantel left onto ledge 25 feet up, ...
traverse right to finish on northeast side.

23 Deleted.

24 F7. Climb 15 feet at east corner, traverse 5 feet ...
left on a ledge, then up south side. The summit ...
band essentially ends with this buttress.

25 Deleted.

26 F7. Corner. Climb uppermost section (obstructed ...
b pine tree) around on north side.

27 REEN SLIME, F9A. A sheer lichen-encrusted ...
wal th a hanging crack. Climb 10 feet straight ...
up t e beginning of the crack; at the crux, stem ...
out to right and get a grip using a thumb jam ...
in the owest part of the crack.

Diagram VII W

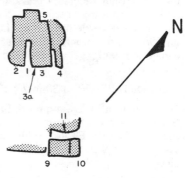

SPLIT TOWER

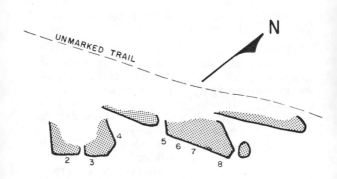

THE BLADE

DIAGRAM VII W

50 FEET

F4. Climb the wide crack to northeast side of the tower. Descend the south crack (easiest), southwest corner, or northwest corner.

F9A. Northeast side just left of the wide crack.

F6. Southeast corner. Mount a block beneath a corner overhang, get around the overhang on the center face.

SECOND PITCH, a 30-foot wall:

F6. Climb small ledges on north half of wall, starting from a detached platform.

PINCH FINGER, F8. An angling crack in the smooth south part of the wall, leading to a shrub and loose block.

THIRD PITCH, a 15-foot wall:

F4. Climb the obvious central crack or climb a chimney on the left.

FOURTH PITCH, a narrow, particularly ridge-like section 40 feet high:

F4. Wide crack in southeast side, starting behind a tree. Climb the crack 25 feet, finish on southeast ledges. Variation, F5. Start in the crack, about 10 feet up traverse right to east corner and climb the corner.

F5. Narrow corner on south side, separated from main ridge by a sloping V-chimney.

F8. Crack in the steep north wall of the ridge. Climb the crack through a niche (delicate layback just above the niche), when crack ends move left to east corner.

There is a humpy slab adjacent to the north wall of the ridge. There are several variations around the left and upper margins of the slab; most of these lead back onto the ridge. One example:

F7. Ascend the slab just past a 5-foot overhang opposite north wall of the ridge. Traverse out (left) along a horizontal chockstone crack above the overhang, then climb the tricky corner above.

FIFTH PITCH, a 20-foot step:

F5. Climb the diagonal crack to the northeast corner.
F4. Walk around south side for other variations.

SIXTH PITCH:

F3. Scramble up the crest of the ridge to platform at base of Turk's Tooth.
F5. On south flank of the ridge there is a niche with two cracks radiating upward; either crack may be followed.

PAT'S RIDGE (no diagram)

There are scattered rocks in a wooded section of the bluff 100 to 300 feet north of Turk's Head Ridge. Several short climbs can be organized into an intermittent sequence that roughly parallels Turk's Head Ridge.

Prospect Point Towers

These towers form a ridge on the middle third of the bluff below Prospect Point. ACCESS: Take Tumbled Rocks Trail north to the 150-foot-wide boulderfield. Ascend the boulders, or a faint path in the trees to the south, to base of the first tower. Several large blocks, with short overhanging chimneys between them (climbable), are encountered a little below the first tower.

FIRST TOWER (Diagram VIII W)

1 Deleted.

2 F6. 25-foot wall at base of First Tower.

3 F5. 15-foot standing block above preceding wall. Climb northeast corner of the block. Southwest side is best way off.

SUN-TOP TOWER (Diagram VIII W)

4 CAN'T-CAN'T, F10A. Start near south corner, climb easily to ledge at 15 feet, traverse left to the pointed nose where a chorus-girl kick can be employed to achieve a stemming position in the wide inside corner, work up the inside corner, go left onto the nose, or continue straight up.

5 THE SUCKER, F7. Climb a short wall with crack leading to a ledge at base of a V-chimney, climb chimney to top. Variation, F6. To avoid lower wall, climb to the ledge at south corner, then move right to the chimney.

6 SUN-TOP, F8. Crack/overhang behind a pine tree, named to commemorate the day this lecherous tree snagged the brief garment worn by a female climber. Climb to ledge below the overhang, work up to reach a good horizontal crack on the left, then bring feet up high while leaning left and reach for handhold in exit crack, climb to top.

7 F7. Northeast ridge. Climb sloping ledges to a small inside corner on east side of the ridge, do one hard move to reach platform above. Variations: Instead of the inside corner, traverse a few feet left to a crack obstructed by tree branches, or go right around to north side of the ridge.

Diagram VIII W

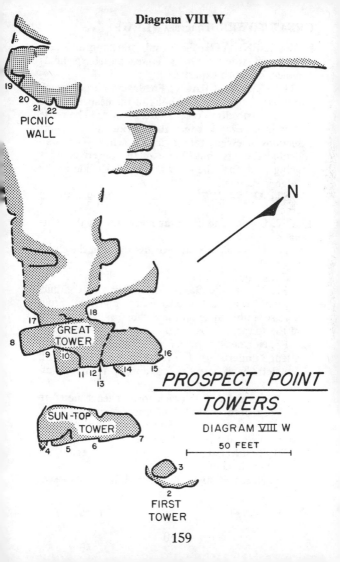

PICNIC WALL

19 20 21 22

N

17 18

GREAT TOWER

8 9 10 11 12 13 14 15 16

PROSPECT POINT TOWERS

DIAGRAM VIII W

50 FEET

SUN-TOP TOWER

4 5 6 7

FIRST TOWER

2 3

GREAT TOWER (Diagram VIII W)

8 GARDEN PATH, F7. Climb overhang and face on south side of Great Tower on sharp holds typical of south exposures.

9 THE GREAT CRACK, F6. Inside corner/crack just left of the large overhang of the east face; this is the classic climb on the Great Tower. The route goes over several ledges that divide it into short sections. Descent route: drop down a short wall behind the east high point of the tower, contour going west until the gully on the south side of the ridge is reached.

10 STEAK SAUCE, A1. Large overhang with aid crack.

11 F7. Corner and crack at north end of the overhang.

12 F8. Thin crack in the face just south of the chimney (13).

13 F4. Chimney.

14 F7. Climb the flake-edge crack and continue straight up a short face to a large platform. From here scramble up ledges and short walls to the top of the tower.

15 F8. Northeast corner. Stay left of the corner until a ledge underneath an overhang is reached. Work out (left) back onto the face and up to main platform.

16 F7. Ascend a wide crack to first ledge noted in 15, step onto a block underneath the overhang, then work somewhat right to reach vertical holds that lead to the platform above.

17 F4. South chimney, an alpine-like route for ascent or descent.

18 F5. North chimney, dirty but long and exposed.

PICNIC WALL (Diagram VIII W)

19 F6. Climb into a niche, traverse out around right corner, and climb to top.

20 F9A. Here is the climb to stretch you out. Secure a beautiful handhold that is just out of reach from the ground, reach far up to the right for the second (not the first) little triangular pocket, continue climbing on widely spaced holds to the overhang above, which should now seem easy.

21 TRACK CRACKS, F8. Climb the parallel cracks, using twin jam holds at the crux 12 feet up.

22 F4. Chimney.

Prospect Point Rampart

ACCESS: Prospect Point is on the West Bluff Trail, ½ mile from south end of the trail. Climbs near Prospect Point are accessible simply by walking down around the south end of the rampart. Climbs farther north can be reached by descending through the Great Chimney or Lost Face access gully. When approaching the area from below, ascend south edge of the 500-foot boulderfield (second large open patch along Tumbled Rocks Trail).

PROSPECT POINT to BIG TOE (Diagram IX W)

1 Deleted.

2-10 Below the south side of Prospect Point there is a group of short routes that offer convenient climbing near the trail. Route 8 (F9A), on a bulging wall, is the most challenging.

11 PROSPECT POINT PINNACLE (northwest side), F4. This small tower is just off the top of the bluff. Start from the saddle between pinnacle and bluff.

Diagram IX W

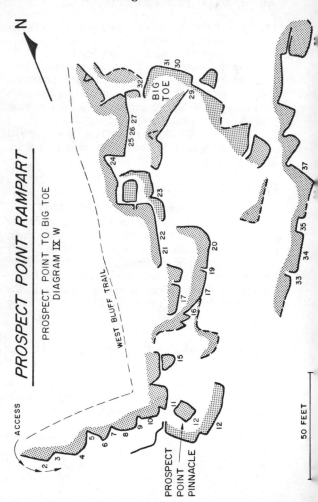

PROSPECT POINT RAMPART

PROSPECT POINT TO BIG TOE
DIAGRAM IX W

162

12 PROSPECT POINT PINNACLE (southeast side), F8. Start on short wall (F7) below southeast side of PPP, climb the wall to platform that supports the tower, up southeast side to a sloping ledge, mantel on south side to reach top.

13, 14 Deleted.

15 F7. Corner of a small tower.

16 F4. Inside corner with crack.

17 F6. Start: two cracks 3 feet apart. Climb either crack (or both) to a platform 25 feet up, ascend some ledges, and complete the climb on the upper wall.

18 Deleted.

19, 20 F4. Broken wall with ledges, mixed climbing and scrambling. Both indicated starts are surprisingly hard considering appearance. On the upper wall finish with 17 or other lines to the north.

21 F5. Crack leading to V-niche.

22 F8. Climb upper wall through two small niches, end with a short crack that diagonals to the right.

23 F7. Slabby inside corner leading to a chimney complex.

24 F5. V-chimney.

25 F7. Start up a thin crack, end a bit left in a chimney with overhanging capstones.

26 F7. Start with a bucket hold on first ledge (4 feet north of preceding crack), mount the ledge and continue slightly right into a big notch. Note: 25 and 26 blend at one point if the easiest climbing is sought.

27 F9A. Overhanging section of lower wall. Start at a short crack, step right onto a ledge 6 feet up, then work up by a jam in the flaring crack above.

28 Deleted.

29 BIG TOE, F4. Start behind a cobra-head tower, climb near east corner of Big Toe onto the large sloping platform.

30 F9A. Crack in northeast side of Big Toe.

31 F7. Flake holds 5 feet right of route 30, F8 if first 8 feet are done directissima.

32 F4. Short chimney, leads onto Big Toe.

DARK WALL (Diagram IX W)

A wall at the base of Prospect Point Rampart, encountered when ascending somewhat north from Prospect Point Towers.

33 F4. Chimney.

34 F6. Wall with ledge halfway up. Climb to south end of the ledge, then up left to top.

35 F4. Wide chimney.

36 SOUL FOOD, F9A. Slightly overhanging face. Climb onto ledge at 10 feet, then up a thin crack to top.

37 F6. Nondescript wall facing northeast.

38 F7. Tower at north end of the Dark Wall; climb the face.

BIG TOE to GREAT CHIMNEY (Diagram X W)

Some of these routes are on the lower half of the cliff, others on the upper half, various combinations forming complete ascents. Ledges separating lower and upper routes are labeled DD to GG on the diagram.

39 F4. Dirty chimney, reaches all the way to the top of the rampart.

40 F6, A1. Start below a pointed nose 20 feet up. Hang a sling from an overhanging crack to gain slab on south side of the nose, climb to top of the nose, then a crack to upper ledge DD. Free-climbing variation, F9A. Start on a rib below the slab,

Diagram X W

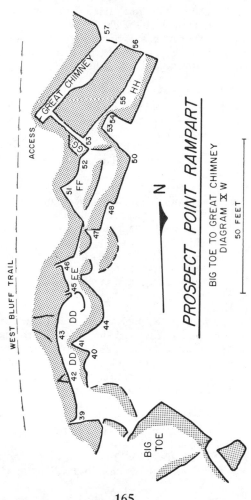

PROSPECT POINT RAMPART

BIG TOE TO GREAT CHIMNEY
DIAGRAM X W

50 FEET

climb 10 feet and step left, then up delicate, lichen-covered rock to a ledge level with top of the nose.

41 F6. Chimney on north side of the pointed nose.

42 GRAND ILLUSION, F8. Crack/overhang above ledge DD. Climb a left-slanting crack toward a notch in the upper wall. Don't go into the notch, which is down-sloping and holdless; instead, traverse left beneath the overhang, climb the overhang and crack to top.

43 F4. A couple of steps lead to a recessed section in the upper wall; this is more or less an escape route from DD.

44 F5. Start in adjacent chimney (41), cross north onto first large ledge and into a small inside corner, scramble up to ledge EE.

45 F7. Crack and notch just north of a corner on the upper wall. (Reach the crack from ledge EE below or by traversing north on DD.)

46 F6. Inside corner with chimney above north end of EE.

47 F5. Climb in a V-chimney, then continue to the right up slabby rock to reach ledge FF.

48 F7. Inside corner and cracks on 30-foot lower wall.

49 Deleted.

50 F5. Start on the outside corner and climb right into a 20-foot crack, passing a 6-foot arrowhead flake, step onto the ledge above, go left around the corner, and scramble to ledge FF (large stump).

51 F5. Inside corner above south end of FF. Variation, F8. Overhanging crack just left of the inside corner.

52 F7. From north end of FF, climb short cracked wall to small platform GG 15 feet below the top, finish on south wall above GG.

53 DOUBLE JEOPARDY, F6. This chimney provides an ascent of the entire wall. Start in south inside corner of a rectangular recessed section, climb chimney past a couple of overhanging chockstones to platform GG, thence to top.

54 STUCK KNEE, F7. Start in north inside corner of the recessed section, climb 15 feet to first ledge, on the same line continue up a crack to base of a narrow chimney, climb chimney (crux) to ledge above, finish by a 12-foot inside corner, or on easy ledges (left).

55 BIVOUAC LEDGE, F7, A1. Start by climbing onto the point of a boulder resting on ledge HH. Climb wall above, following a crack past an overhang to the bivouac ledge, then up a wider crack at north end of the ledge.

56 SON OF GREAT CHIMNEY, F10A. A hideous promontory, suggestive of The End on the East Bluff. From ledge HH, cross over to northeast corner of the promontory, go around corner and up north wall to a cramped ledge, up overhanging crack (crux) a few feet to handholds at the level of Bivouac Ledge (to which escape is possible), traverse right and grasp a welcome rock prong at northwest corner, climb corner to top.

57 GREAT CHIMNEY, F4. A frequently used access route. There is a steep part at the bottom that is a little tricky.

GREAT CHIMNEY to LOST FACE (Diagram XI W)

58 F4. Chimney.

59 F5. Chimney with overhang.

60 HANDLE WITH CARE, F6. Climb the flaky crack to a platform, continue in a short chimney to top.

61 F8. Start on face near chimney (62), move left to a ledge, follow crack to platform above.

62 F6. Narrow chimney. Staying outside the chimney makes for better climbing.

Diagram XI W

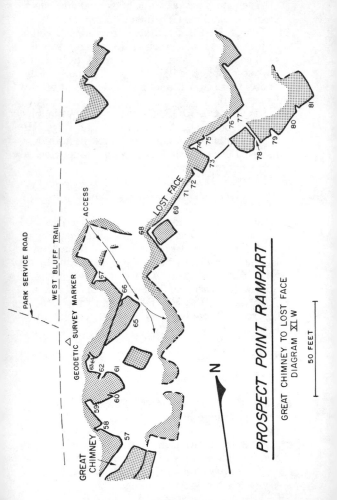

PROSPECT POINT RAMPART

GREAT CHIMNEY TO LOST FACE
DIAGRAM XI W

50 FEET

168

63 F7. Dirty crack. Start 3 feet right of chimney (62).
64 F6. Crack.
65 F7. Climb an obvious 30-foot crack to top of a huge block, climb 10 feet (crux) to next ledge, continue more easily to top of wall.
66 F5. Narrow chimney.
67 F5. Inside corner with crack.
68 F4. Start behind a 25-foot tower at base of Lost Face, climb easy rock and ledges tending to the south, ending in upper part of access gully.
69 LOST FACE, F6. Longest climb on the West Bluff. Start on a slanting ledge, climb crack system that leads fairly directly into a niche in the center of the face, continue up the inside corner of the niche and on ledges, ending at a large ledge on south side of summit boulder. LOST FACE OVERHANG, F8. Before reaching the niche traverse left under the overhang, surmount it by a crack 12 feet south of the niche, continue straight up to the large ledge as above.
70 Deleted.
71 F7. Thin crack that splits 15 feet up; left crack joins route 69, right crack ends at a walk-off halfway up north edge of the face.
72 F10A. Smooth section of the face between the crack (71) and north edge. The route continues onto a narrow bulge 40 feet up.
73 F8. Separate steep slab. Delicate, especially upper part near north edge.
74 F5. Chimney.
75 F8. Start in niche, ascend overhang and crack above.
76 F7. Crack at north end of small overhang.
77 F4. Crack, used as access route.
78-81 Short chimneys and faces.

RECLINING TOWER (Diagram XII W)

Reclining Tower and Dead Tree Wall are respectively 150 and 400 feet north of the geodetic marker on the West Bluff Trail. There is an access gully leading down from the trail just south of each formation.

1 F4. Broken ledges.

2 F6. Start under overhang, continue in crack above.

3 Deleted.

4 F7. South side of corner.

5 X-RATED, F10B. Start near northeast corner, climb 8 feet left to a flake under an overhang, move right toward corner, jump for a small projection and retable onto it.

6 Deleted.

7 F7. Climb east corner to base of tower, balance up left onto south corner of the tower, from its top step over a gap to climb another short wall.

8 F7. Climb crack and V-chimney 25 feet onto right-hand ledge, retable to next ledge, continue up and right to third ledge (crux) and top.

9 F6. Two large flakes. Climb north edge of the flakes to join route 8.

10 F5. Chimney on south side of Reclining Tower. There is one point where one can squeeze behind the tower to reach the north side (route 12).

11 RECLINING TOWER ARETE, F6. Start on climb 12, at 20 feet traverse to platform on east corner, climb the arete in two stages to top of Reclining Tower. A more indirect start: from ledge at base of south chimney (10) traverse right behind pine tree to northeast corner of the tower, up corner to platform noted above.

11A F8. Start from the ground, climb crack and overhang to pine tree 15 feet up.

12 F6. North side of Reclining Tower. Climb inside corner and deep awkward crack to top of the tower.

13-15 Short climbs.

Diagram XII W

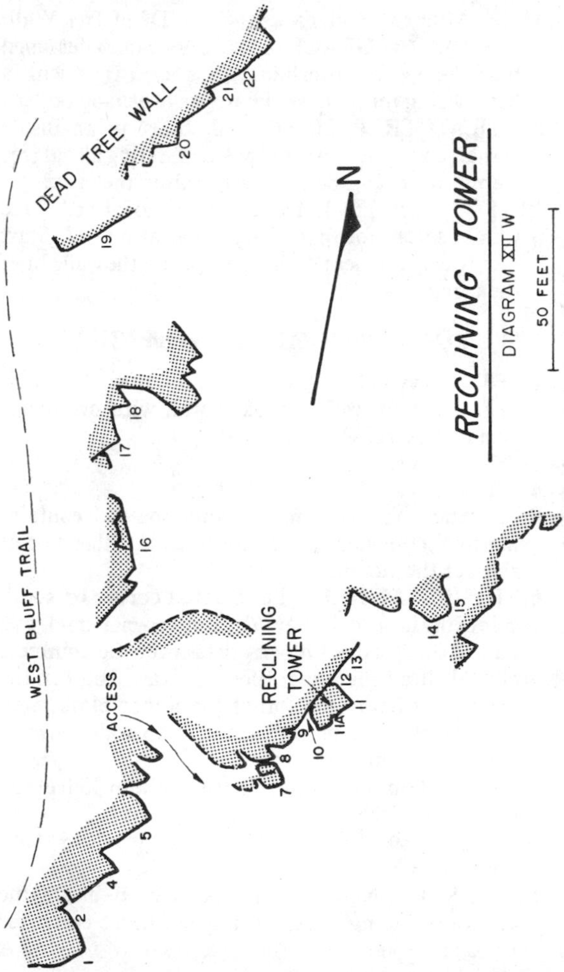

RECLINING TOWER

DIAGRAM XII W

50 FEET

N

DEAD TREE WALL

WEST BLUFF TRAIL

ACCESS

RECLINING TOWER

DEAD TREE WALL (Diagram XII W)

16-19 Minor summit rocks south of Dead Tree Wall.

20 AMAZING GRACE, F9A. Climb onto detached block below first overhang, pass it on right with a hair-raising move, pass the upper overhang on left.

21 DEAD TREE CLIMB, F8. Start in an inside corner, continue in wide crack containing an old tree stump; overhang below the stump is the crux.

22 F9C. Thin crack 10 feet north of Dead Tree Climb, severe for first 10 feet. Variation, F7. Start more easily farther north, continue on the wall above the crack.

CAVE ROCKS RAMPART (Diagram XIII W)

1 F3. Access gully.

2 F7. Cracked, rather broken wall with overhangs (some loose rock).

3 F8. Corner.

4 F5. Crack.

5 F6. Start in short chimney, climb to notch containing tree, continue up on the outside either left or right of the notch.

6 THE CLAMSHELL, F6. Start at corner on south side of the large chimney (7), climb corner crack to a pair of sharp-edged blocks that cover the chimney, climb behind the upper block or crawl between the two; 4 feet below the top of the upper block, step over (south) to a platform, finish on wall above.

7 F4. Large chimney.

8 F6. Start on south side of corner, climb 15 feet, go right around corner and up.

9 SOUTH ENCLOSURE, F7. Climb inside by stemming or layback.

10 NORTH ENCLOSURE, F6. Climb inside the enclosure facing north, using left-hand crack for layback.

11-13 Short climbs.

Diagram XIII W

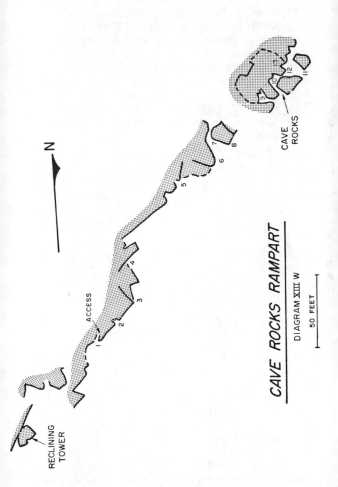

CAVE ROCKS RAMPART

DIAGRAM XIII W

50 FEET

CAVE ROCKS

RECLINING TOWER

ACCESS

N

HANGMAN TOWERS (no diagram)

There are scattered rocks which deserve some mention 100-500 feet north of the Dead Tree Wall. It is convenient to start the description at the lower level and proceed upward.

The lowest climbs are located by reference to a landmark boulder, The Turtle. This can be reached from Tumbled Rocks Trail (see West Bluff approaches). From The Turtle ascend about 100 feet to the first few climbing rocks, roughly at mid-level on the bluff. Two routes here:

THE HANGMAN, F7. Deep inside corner and crack with overhang. Where the crack runs through the overhang it appears possible to hang by one's head; a better technique, however, is to use an incredibly dirty chockstone.

F6. Southeast side of The Hangman. The climb starts from a block.

From The Hangman walk up (slightly south) 150 feet to the base of the TWIN RIDGE. The north and south ridges are separated by a narrow gully, with the north ridge starting from the lower level.

NORTH TWIN RIDGE, F5. Four or five short pitches, starting with two towers and a short wall that leads to a back-sloping platform ("lunch spot"), a point about 100 feet off the summit.

KNOBBY PILLAR, F5. A narrow tower 50 feet south of the lunch spot. Start at the south corner or climb the more difficult north overhang (F8).

SOUTH TWIN RIDGE, F6. The base of the south ridge is a pair of detached blocks. Chimney up behind the lower block (tricky start) to base of an imposing section, continue on south side of the south ridge.

NOWHERE LEDGE, F9C. Start below the imposing section of the south ridge, step onto a diagonal crack, move right and climb a few feet near northeast corner, continue to platform above.

F9A. North side of south ridge. Climb a cul-de-sac chimney into a hanging inside corner, up corner to top.

BIRD BATH TOWER, F8. A 25-foot tower 60 feet south of the upper part of the Twin Ridge. Climb northeast side of the tower, using the (seemingly) innocuous ledge halfway up.

From the base of the Twin Ridge go south about 100 feet (crossing a low rock ridge with an extended southeast face) to reach The Beast, a 15-foot block sitting on a pedestal.

F5. Climb the obvious inside corner on the east side of the pedestal, then climb the northeast corner of the block.

F6-F7. A compact group of towers 40 feet south of The Beast, with two or three routes.

GO-GO TOWER, F7. This tower is 70 feet north of the lunch spot on the Twin Ridge. Climb the southeast corner, an interesting layback with dynamic moves.

F9A. Overhanging ledges on east side of Go-Go Tower.

From Go-Go Tower follow a faint path angling down and north to a band of rocks 80 feet long. The area is about a third of the way down the bluff, 200 feet north of the Twin Ridge.

F7. Tower at upper (south) end of the band. Climb a V-chimney that starts above the first ledge; avoid the little platform on north side of the chimney.

THE PORPOISE, F5. A narrow fin-shaped structure at the lower (north) end of the band, easily climbed on the ridge, which is more solid than it appears.

F7. North side of The Porpoise. Difficulty may depend on how resolutely one stays on the face.

F8. The center section of the band consists of two shapeless buttresses. Climb south middle buttress at south corner or on southeast face.

F7. Climb north middle buttress at southeast corner.

TREE TOWER (Diagram XIV W)

ACCESS: West Bluff Trail, about ⅔ of the way to the north end of the lake. Locate a small boulderfield that reaches almost to the trail; the Tree Tower is 200 feet north of the boulderfield. A steep rock access gully in the wall just behind the tower can be used to descend from the trail.

1 TREE TOWER (east ridge), F7. The traditional route on the tower. Start near lowest point, climb ledges on the ridge to an inside corner on northeast side, climb this difficult corner (which has a peculiar rock splinter) to top. Descend at a flake on south side of the tower (4).

2 F4. Southeast side, broken by very favorable vertical holds.

3 F8. North side. Start just left of the obtuse north corner, climb up and a little left onto a block, then up a short crack to the pine tree.

5 BOWLER'S GRIP, F8. Climb the northwest side of the Tree Tower, using (if possible) the two finger-holes below the upper horizontal crack.

6 F8. Climb just left of small overhang on the wall above the Tree Tower.

7 F8. This line goes directly up the small overhang of route 6.

8 F7. Corner adjacent to access gully.

9 F5. Ledges adjacent to the corner on north side of access gully.

10-14 F4-F6. Generally moderate chimneys and corners.

Diagram XIV W

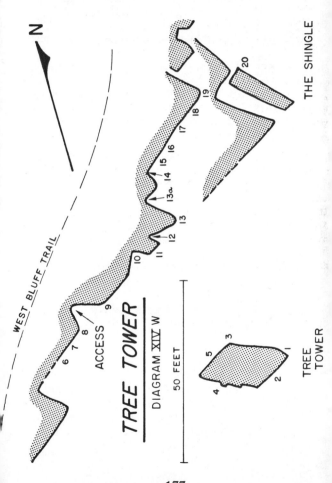

N

WEST BLUFF TRAIL

ACCESS

6 7 8

9

10

11 12

13

13a 14

15 16 17

18 19

20

THE SHINGLE

TREE TOWER
DIAGRAM XIV W

50 FEET

TREE TOWER

3

5

4

2

1

15 F5. Layback crack.

16 F7. Crack, mostly finger and toe jams. Cracks 15 and 16 are only a couple of feet apart, but are most interesting if kept as separate routes.

17 F9A. Face with thin crack.

18 F8. Another thin crack, this one passing a small overhang.

19 KOALA BEAR, F10A. Shinny up corner using holds on both sides.

20 THE SHINGLE, F9A. A narrow vertical formation below the main wall. Climb northwest corner, adjacent to the gap at west end of the formation.

A summit wall (no diagram) 150 feet south of the Tree Tower projects over the boulderfield to a sharp corner of clear rock 30 feet high.

DER SCHNOZZEL, F8. Start on right side of the corner or from a boulder on left side. Step up onto the corner, climb from ledge to ledge to a rock divot on right side (please use carefully and replace for next climber) and then to top.

CAKE WALK, F9A. Start on south side of the corner, climb the smooth face to a crack, up crack to top.

F5-F6. There are a few more inside corner and face climbs on the same wall, 20-40 feet south of the corner.

TYROLEAN TOWER (no diagram)

The TYROLEAN TOWER is 200 feet north of the Tree Tower, below an elevated vantage point along the crest of the bluff (short rise in trail when approaching from south). Descend about 100 feet to reach base of the tower.

F3. An easy chimney on the south side leads into the gap behind the 20-foot summit block of the tower.

F6. Start 10-15 feet right of the easy chimney, climb a crack up and left into the gap. Variation, F6. Climb partway up the crack as above, then traverse right and climb up to north platform (level with gap behind the tower).

F8. Start in gap, on southwest side of the summit block; climb a thin crack 5 feet, move right onto south corner where top of tower is easy. Variation, F9A. Continue straight up above the thin crack.

F5, A1. Start on north platform (noted above), climb north side (using stirrup) to top of tower.

F6-F7. The wall just south of Tyrolean Tower has two routes.

There is a summit buttress 500 feet north of the Tyrolean Tower, not visible from the trail. It is necessary to walk about 25 feet east from the trail to reach the top of the buttress.

PEARLY GATE, F9A. Obvious inside corner on east side of the buttress.

F7. North side of the buttress. Climb a crack leading to a creaking block.

INCH WORM, F8. Another outcropping, at a lower level 150 feet south of Pearly Gate. Climb a shallow inside corner past north end of overhang on southeast side of the outcropping.

BY GULLY (no diagram)

These rocks are ¼ mile from the north end of the West Bluff Trail (trail terminus is along entrance road to north shore area). The trail passes the head of a large dirt gully with an outcropping on the north side 100 feet down.

F6. Climb south corner of first buttress, adjacent to the gully. (The southeast side of this buttress is a forbidding overhanging wall.)

F8. North side of first buttress. Climb to niche, proceed left or right of the nose above.

F7. Inside corner on south side of second buttress.

F9A. Southeast face of second buttress. Climb near left (south) corner or on right side of the face.

HOLLYWOOD AND VINES (no diagram)

This summit band extends 400 feet along the West Bluff Trail. The region is directly above the north shore of the lake. Perhaps the best climbing of the band is on the southernmost buttress, about 80 feet from where the rocks first arise along the summit.

F6. Southeast side of south buttress is a V-chimney with a wide crack. Climb on the left side of the "V" or (better) climb the right crack, first as a chimney and then on the outside when the crack narrows and finally splits.

F7. Corner of south buttress. Start just left of corner, finish via a layback crack on the right (north) side.

F7. North side of south buttress. Climb blocks leading to a wider crack, jam your way up the crack (requires a good-sized fist).

F8. The next buttress to the north has clean-looking rock. Start up on the north side, traverse around east corner to a ledge on south side, finish on a smooth delicate face.

F7. Continuing north, there is a large oak tree growing at an unnatural angle across a wall, blocking a couple of potential routes. You can start in the middle of one climb by walking up the trunk.

F6. Proceeding north from the oak tree, there is a somewhat lower-angle wall with two or three large flakes. The route follows these flakes.

F7. A corner accentuated by a reddish rib or prominence. Climb the corner to an overhanging crack that luckily contains a chockstone (albeit a loose one).

F8. Corner just south of a pronounced recessed section. Climb the corner, using a projecting rock finger for a foothold, followed by an overhanging crack.

In the recessed section there is a point of access to the trail above. Opposite this section there are two adjacent small towers, the east one vine-covered (this is Hollywood). The harder route on each is on the east side. Broken summit rocks continue north for another 150 feet.

THE BOTTOM is a hidden spot below the branch trail that runs parallel to the base of Hollywood and Vines. Where this trail draws even with the south end of Hollywood and Vines, a short ridge extends downward (east) about 100 feet, terminating abruptly in a wall 30 feet high and 40 feet wide. The wall has three climbs:

F5. Climb the central crack, step right to a small pine tree to finish.

LEFT CHEEK, F8. On south half of the wall. Climb a slight rib with a small overhang near top.

RIGHT CHEEK, F9A. North half of the wall. This is a fuzzy route on down-sloping ledges.

NORTH SLOPE (no diagram)

The last rock band along the summit trail, 375 feet from the north end of the trail. The elevation of the bluff here (as you proceed north) is decreasing rather rapidly; the trail follows some slabs along the edge of the bluff. It is convenient to describe this band from north to south, using buttresses as references:

F5. Buttress I (at north end) is behind a large dead pine tree. Climb the north side.

F5-F6. Southeast side of buttress II is a nice face climb with variations.

F7. Buttress III is less pronounced than II or IV. Climb the corner, starting as a layback on northeast side.

F4. Access chimney on south side of III.

F7. Overhanging ledges at the northeast corner of buttress IV.

F5. Southeast side of IV, a moderate wall.

There are rocks continuing 50 feet to the south at a slightly lower level. The first (north) section is a wall with mostly bucket holds, though it is difficult to start at the lowest point. To the south (past a wide crack and an inside corner) there is a smooth narrow wall with vertical joints, an attractive face climb (F8). The south side of this wall is a flake climb with an old piton. The rocks farther south seem to offer little of interest.

THE SOUTH BLUFF

The South Bluff is practically devoid of interest to climbers and is rarely visited. At one time there was a South Bluff Trail; now it can hardly be found over most of the bluff. One of the most rewarding features at the South Bluff is the superb view of the lake and the East and West Bluffs.

There is only one set of outcroppings, consisting of several small towers located in the boulderfield near the top of the bluff east of the campground. There are three main towers on the South Bluff, approximately across the valley from the Leaning Tower. A few short climbs can be made on these towers. At the base of the bluff below these towers is an old quarry cut which contains natural springs. In the winter the drainage from these springs builds up short ice walls useful for ice climbing practice. The springs dry up after a succession of dry summers, but recover after a summer of normal rainfall.

Inasmuch as the South Bluff is infrequently visited by hikers and climbers, the likelihood of encountering a rattlesnake should not be overlooked.

BIBLIOGRAPHY

Armstrong, Patricia. 1966. "Devil's Lake, Geological Showplace of the Midwest." *Earth Science* (May-June), pp. 112-115.

Armstrong, Patricia K. S. 1968. *Cryptogram Communities on Quartzite of Devil's Lake, Wisconsin.* M.S. thesis, University of Chicago.

Black, Robert F. 1964. "Potholes and Associated Gravel of Devil's Lake State Park." *Wisconsin Academy of Sciences, Arts and Letters* 53: 165-175.

Black, Robert F. 1965. "Ice-wedge Casts of Wisconsin." *Wisconsin Academy of Sciences, Arts and Letters* 54: 187-222.

Black, Robert F. 1967-68. "Geomorphology of Devil's Lake Area, Wisconsin." *Wisconsin Academy of Sciences, Arts and Letters* 56: 117-148.

Blackshaw, Alan. 1973. *Mountaineering.* 3d ed. Baltimore, Md.: Penguin Books.

Curtis, John T. 1959. *The Vegetation of Wisconsin.* Madison: The University of Wisconsin Press.

Dalziel, I. W. D., R. H. Dott, Jr., R. F. Black, and J. H. Zimmerman. 1970. *Geology of the Baraboo District, Wisconsin.* Geology and Natural History Survey Information Circular no. 14, Madison, Wisconsin.

Fassett, Norman C. 1931. *Spring Flora of Wisconsin.* Madison: The University of Wisconsin Press.

Ferber, Peggy, ed. 1975. *Mountaineering: The dom of the Hills.* 3d ed. Seattle, Wash.: The taineers.

Lange, Kenneth I., and Ralph T. Tuttle. *Lake Where Spirits Live: A Human Hi Midwest's Most Popular Park.* Ba Baraboo Printing.

Primak, William. 1965. *Guidebook to the Local Practice Climbing Areas of the Chicago Mountaineering Club, Devil's Lake Section.* Chicago, Ill.: Chicago Mountaineering Club.

Reidel Arthur, ed. 1973. *Fundamental Rock Climbing.* 2d ed. Cambridge, Mass.: The M.I.T. Outing Club.

Robbins, Royal. 1971. *Basic Rockcraft.* Glendale, Calif.: La Siesta Press.

Robbins, Royal. 1973 *Advanced Rockcraft.* Glendale, Calif.: La Siesta Press.

Smith, David, and Roger Zimmerman. 1970. *Climbers and Hikers Guide to Devil's Lake.* Madison: Wisconsin Hoofers.

INDEX OF CLIMBS

191

DESIGNED BY GARDNER R. WILLS
COMPOSED BY
FOX VALLEY TYPESETTING, MENASHA, WISCONSIN
MANUFACTURED BY
BANTA DIVISION, GEORGE BANTA COMPANY, INC.,
MENASHA, WISCONSIN
TEXT AND DISPLAY LINES ARE SET IN TIMES ROMAN

Library of Congress Cataloging in Publication Data
Widule, William.
Climber's guide to Devil's Lake.
"Preparation of this guide was sponsored by the
Chicago Mountaineering Club."
Bibliography: p.
Includes index.
1. Rock climbing—Wisconsin—Devil's Lake—Guide-
books. 2. Devil's Lake, Wisc.—Description and travel—
Guide-books. I. Swartling, Sven Olof. II. Chicago
Mountaineering Club. III. Title.
GV199.42.W62D488   796.5'22'0977576   78-65018
ISBN 0-299-07804-3

NOTES